GOING
deeper

A Discipleship Model on the Gospel of Luke

DR. O'SHEA LOWERY

innovo PUBLISHING
innovopublishing.com

Published by Innovo Publishing, LLC
www.innovopublishing.com
1-888-546-2111

innovo
PUBLISHING
innovopublishing.com

Publishing quality books, eBooks, audiobooks, music, screenplays & courses for the Christian & wholesome markets since 2008.

GOING DEEPER
(Leader's Guide)
A Discipleship Model on the Gospel of Luke

BOOK 2
THE STRONG & COURAGEOUS SINGLE MOMS SERIES

Library of Congress Control Number: 2024931573
ISBN: 978-1-61314-985-0

Cover Design & Interior Layout: Innovo Publishing, LLC

Printed in the United States of America
U.S. Printing History
First Edition: 2024

Has God called you to create a Christ-centered or wholesome book, eBook, audiobook, music album, screenplay, or online course? Visit Innovo's educational center (cpportal.com) to learn how to accomplish your calling with excellence.

Throughout my years, I have been blessed to be surrounded by godly individuals who poured into my life in ways that aided my growth as a Christian. Those individuals were men and women of great character and integrity. They were dedicated prayer warriors, steadfast in their faith, and devoted to serving others. They were people who were trustworthy, safe, and filled with the love of Jesus Christ.

I dedicate this book to such persons, with a heart of gratitude and thanksgiving for all they have done for my life. Thank you for investing in me, for loving me, and for teaching me how to follow Jesus. You are and have been one of the greatest blessings in my life!

—Dr. O'Shea Lowery

Dr. O'Shea Lowery is well qualified to write *Going Deeper*, a 24-week discipleship model based on the book of Luke, teaching the reader how to study, treasure, and obey God's Word. The book is designed for a small group, in which the leader enables participants to grow spiritually through prayer, homework, studying the Bible, and meeting together once a week. Shea takes to heart 2 Timothy 2:2:

> *The things which you have heard from me in the presence of many witnesses, entrust these to faithful men who will be able to teach others also.*

As Shea's pastor for a number of years, I enthusiastically recommend this discipleship study.

—Dr. Robert Jeffress, Senior Pastor, First Baptist Church, Dallas, TX

Contents

Segment 1: Luke 1–12

Segment 2: Luke 13–24

Introduction to the
Going Deeper Study

Welcome to *Going Deeper*, a 24-week discipleship model. We are thrilled you have decided to commit to this study.

As I look back on my journey, I recall several people who God used to disciple me, even when I did not understand the concept of being discipled. These individuals had a huge influence on my life in many areas.

- They discipled me with the Word of God.
- They taught me the importance of God's Word and how it will change my life.
- They taught me the importance of obeying and aligning my life with the Word of God while helping me to understand it more clearly.
- They opened up their lives, as well as their homes, to listen when I needed to talk, to encourage when I had days of struggle, and to offer biblical guidance when I searched for answers.
- They taught me through example about prayer as they prayed for me and with me.
- They taught me about the importance of accountability.

Where Did All These Discipleship Moments Take Place?

They took place in a variety of settings—at church, in small groups, within homes, at restaurants, on walking trails, on the telephone, and through various other avenues. They were in Bible study settings as well as in moments of fellowship. (Note: fellowship moments are great, but if we try and disciple only through fellowship, leaving out the Word of God, this is not true discipleship.)

As individuals did life with me, I watched how they parented, and I watched how they responded to situations that arose. I watched how they made Jesus the center of their lives and of their decisions. I watched how they poured into the lives of others, including my own, and I watched them die to themselves while serving others. Now I think it is important to note here that these individuals were Christians bearing fruit, faithful church attendees, spiritually healthy, and growing in the Lord.

So, What Is Discipleship?

Robby Gallaty, senior pastor of Long Hollow Baptist Church in Hendersonville, Tennessee, sums it up when he states, "Discipleship is intentionally equipping believers with the Word of God through accountable relationships empowered by the Holy Spirit in order to replicate faithful followers of Christ."[1] Discipling others in this manner enable us to fulfill Christ's commands. In Matthew 28:19-20, Jesus said, "Go therefore and make disciples of all the nations, baptizing them in the name of the Father and the Son and the Holy Spirit, teaching them to observe all that I commanded you; and lo, I am with you always, even to the end of the age." Jesus calls us to go and to make disciples. Through the study of *Going Deeper*, we are doing just that. How? This discipleship will begin with a small group but extend beyond it as well.

[1.] Robby Gallaty & Chris Swain, *Replicate: How to Create a Culture of Disciple-Making Right Where You Are* (Chicago, IL: Moody Publishers, 2020).

What Is Going Deeper?

Going Deeper is a 24-week discipleship model based on the book of Luke and taught in two, 12-week segments. In a small group discipleship setting, single moms (and otherse alike) will be taught how to study, treasure, and obey God's Word, while participating in Bible study/homework, scripture memorization, small group fellowship/accountability, and prayer.

The following leader guide gives instructions for those individuals desiring to start and lead a discipleship group in the *Going Deeper* study.

Leader's Guide Instructions

Welcome, leaders! I am so glad you have agreed to serve in the role as leader for the *Going Deeper* discipleship group. Whether your desire is to start or teach a group—or both—we are here to cheer you on, to pray for you, and to guide you toward the necessary steps to take both in starting a group and completing one.

How to Begin a *Going Deeper* Discipleship Group: Pray, Prepare, Plan, Participate, and Partner

Pray

As you commit to the Lord your desire to either start or teach a group—or both—engage in the following actions: (1) Pray for the Lord to lead you through all aspects of starting this group. (2) Pray for His timing on when to start the group. (3) Pray for God to put together your cluster of ladies. (4) Enlist others to join you in praying for you as you lead and for those who you will be leading.

Prepare (Yourself)

As you seek the Lord for His direction and timing and for the group of ladies you will study with, do your homework. Learn everything you can about the *Going Deeper* study—what you will need in the startup, in the continuation of, and in the completion of the study. In addition, know what is expected not only of the teacher but of the students as well. Next, prepare yourself through prayer, Bible study, meditation, and listening to the Holy Spirit's voice. Last, as you prepare, commit to see this mission all the way to fruition. Be faithful to God to complete what He has called you to do. You may start out with five ladies, but as it draws to a close, you may only have one remaining. Be as faithful to the one as you were to the entire five. Finish strong.

> *"For which one of you, when he wants to build a tower, does not first sit down and calculate the cost, to see if he has enough to complete it? Otherwise, when he has laid a foundation and is not able to finish, all who are watching it will begin to ridicule him, saying, 'This person began to build, and was not able to finish!'" (Luke 14:28-30)*

Plan

Once the Lord, as well as your church leadership, has given you the green light to proceed, begin making plans for all you will need to start your *Going Deeper* discipleship group. Remember: this study is a 24-week discipleship model, taught in two, 12-week segments. Start with the first segment. Then, after your group completes the first segment, you can offer the next segment to those who desire to continue.

Putting your group together: Pray for the group of ladies that God will place in your small group. (Keep it small, three to five people, so that you can pour into them, fellowship with them, disciple them, and minister to them individually on a weekly basis.) Ask God to lead you to this group of ladies, or ask Him to lead them to you. Note: This is intended to be a closed group, meaning the three to five ladies you start with are the only ones attending through the finish. Once you have met your three to five ladies goal, guard against allowing additional people to flow in and out of this specific group. If you have started the study and have ladies who want to come weeks into it, lead them to another Bible study group within your church, but keep their names so you can invite them when you start over. Or you can pray and enlist other leaders who may want to start an additional *Going Deeper* discipleship study.

Once your group has been established:

1. Order your *Going Deeper* resources: this *Leader's Guide* edition and a *Student Workbook* for each participant.
2. Set a date to begin.
3. Set a place to hold the weekly meetings (within the church or outside the church in someone's home). The location should have access to a TV for optional slide presentations, an audio player, and internet accessibility.

4. Set a starting time and an ending time.
5. Obtain additional supplies the ladies may need, such as pens, Bibles, and paper.
6. Plan the type of refreshments you will serve, if you choose to do so.
7. Start!

Participate

If you are the teacher of the group, be willing to be "all in" as you begin the group, participating in all the necessary requirements of the study, such as weekly attendance, Bible study/homework, memorizing scripture, accountability, prayer, and confidentiality. You are the leader; therefore, it is imperative to set an example. Ask not of others what you are unwilling to do. Lead by example.

First meeting: Your first meeting will be the kick-off of the *Going Deeper* study. You can choose whether or not you'd like to serve refreshments or a meal. This is up to each leader.

Agenda for first meeting:

1. Open up with a welcome.
2. Allow the group some time to get to know one another.
3. Give each lady time to share her name, where she is from, how many children she has (if applicable), and what she enjoys to do in her spare time.
4. Introduce the *Going Deeper* study.
5. Go over the instructions located in the first part of the book with the ladies in your group.
6. Go over what is expected of them, and explain in detail about weekly attendance, Bible study/homework, memorizing scripture, prayer, accountability, and confidentiality.
7. Open discussion for any questions.
8. Introduce the ladies to how the weekly Bible study/homework is to be implemented. Explain there are five days of homework, and they may choose whichever day to begin.
9. At the end of the week when you come back together, the group will discuss the week's lesson.

Weekly meetings: After the first meeting, leaders can conduct their subsequent weekly meetings with their small groups in two ways:

1. Plan (A) agenda: Leaders, you can teach on the chapter studied the previous week for about twenty to twenty-five minutes, then spend the rest of the time with your small groups, asking questions for each day's homework. Those questions consist of the following:
   a. What passage spoke to you the most on day one?
   b. How can we apply what we learned on this day to our lives? *(Leader, help your students understand how to apply Scripture.)*
   c. What did you learn about the character of God within the passage studied? *(This is one of the most important questions. This study will help them to see how God responded to people, situations, crises, sickness, those in the pits of sin, prayer, and so forth. If we know the character of God, we are better able to trust Him.)*
2. Plan (B) agenda: Leaders, you can do an overview of the chapter and then get right into the time with your small groups, asking questions from each day's homework—as mentioned previously.

Partner

Leader, lock arms with your ladies! Over the next six months (or two, 12-week segments), your group will be your mission field. Praying for them and reaching out and encouraging them, as well as fellowshipping with them outside the normal class setting is imperative.

Remember:

- *Pray for your ladies.* Leaders, make sure to spend time praying over your ladies.
- *Contact:* Within the scope of these 12/24 weeks, make sure to reach out to your ladies weekly, either via phone, text, mail, or email. Mix these up, as you do not always want to contact them the same way. At times, they will need to talk. Other times, they will enjoy receiving a card or a simple text or email.

- *Plan special outings with your group.* Some of the greatest discipling takes place as moms do life with you. They will watch you parent your kids or grandkids, they will learn how you handle life by observing how you treat the server at a restaurant, they will note the shows you watch at your home and the music to which you listen. Without knowing it, you will be discipling your ladies as you do life together. *Suggestions:* Invite them to your home for a meal or an afternoon dessert. Ask your ladies to meet you at a restaurant, Dutch treat. Sit together at church. Go on a picnic. Be creative in doing life with your ladies. You can meet with them individually or as a group.

The goals of discipleship are to become more like Jesus, growing in obedience to His teachings; to transform hearts and lives through the power of the Holy Spirit and the Word of God; and to not only be discipled but to also turn around and make disciples.

Leaders, one of the greatest things you will witness in those you will disciple is their turning around and passing on what they have learned as they disciple others. How will you know when they are ready? Watch for the fruit of the Spirit—spiritual growth. Watch for faithfulness—a pattern of perseverance, of not quitting. Watch for a love for God's Word and for His people. And watch for a commitment to the local church.

Student Expectations

Weekly attendance, Bible study/homework, memorizing scripture, accountability to your group, praying for one another, and confidentiality—this is what is expected of the students during this study.

- *Weekly attendance:* Attendance is particularly important in the *Going Deeper* study. When Jesus taught His disciples, they were always present with Him, walking, talking, listening, and learning. Life happens, as we all know and understand, but as much as it depends on them, commit to weekly attendance.

- *Bible study/homework:* This is an imperative step in the journey of discipleship. Commit to engaging in the study of God's Word and in the completion of your homework. Once obeyed, God's Word will transform your heart and your life. Bible study births growth, equipping us for every good work. We learn who God is and of His love for us. Faithfully commit to Bible study and homework.

- *Memorizing scripture:* God tells us in His Word to hide His Word in our hearts. You can memorize scripture in many ways: You can read over it several times throughout the day; you can meditate on it throughout your day, allowing it to take root and bear fruit within your heart and mind; or you can ask the Holy Spirit to speak to you through the passage you are memorizing and to help you obey what it is telling you to do.

- *Accountability to my group:* Mutually holding each other accountable throughout the study of *Going Deeper* is important in order to encourage one another toward growth and toward meeting those goals of weekly attendance, homework, scripture memory, prayer, and confidentiality. (Note: Do this with kindness and a gentle spirit after first humbly confessing your own sins to God.)

- *Praying for one another:* This is a commitment from each person to pray for one another within the group setting as well as independently for each other's special prayer requests.

- *Confidentiality:* Keeping confidence within the group is imperative, unless it is an emergency that needs reporting. If no emergency, at all costs, keep all prayer requests within your group setting. All members must cultivate a safe environment within your group so that everyone feels able to open up to one another.

Thank you again for being willing to participate in the *Going Deeper Discipleship Study* and for being a part of this discipleship family. God's Word will certainly change your life and transform your heart. Remember, start strong and finish strong. Let's get started!

Commitment

As you begin this study, consider the commitment pledge below and its significance to your personal experience through this study.

I commit to the next 12 weeks of *Going Deeper* through engaging in the following: (1) weekly attendance, (2) completion of Bible study/homework, (3) scripture memorization, (4) accountability to my group, (5) praying for members of my group, and (6) confidentiality.

Name: _____

Date: _____

Weeks 1–12

The Gospel of Luke 1-12

Segment 1

Notes

Week 1

Scripture Memory
And blessed is she who believed that there would be a fulfillment of what had been spoken to her by the Lord. (Luke 1:45)

Prayer
Lord Jesus, I come before you during this time of study, asking You to open my heart to hear Your Word and obey Your truth. In Jesus' name I pray, amen.

Scripture Reading By Day
Truth Revealed: What truths did God reveal to you through today's scripture reading? What did God say to you—to your heart—as you read today's scripture?

Truth Applied: How will you use what God revealed to you today in your daily life?

>**Day 1.** Luke 1:1-25

Leader Notes

Focus Points: (a.) The writer is Luke, inspired by the Holy Spirit. (b.) Gabriel's visit to Zacharias, announcing the coming of John. (c.) John's calling announced—as the forerunner before the Lord. (d.) The unbelief of Zacharias and what it cost him. (e.) Elizabeth's realization of the favor of God upon her life.

Revelation: Within the passages studied, ask the ladies to discuss the following: (a.) truths revealed about God's character, (b.) truths revealed that both ministered to and encouraged their hearts, (c.) truths that brought conviction of sin and/or need of change, (d.) truths revealing God's promises, and (e.) truths revealed that restored hope.

Application: Foster to the ladies the importance of applying what they learned of the character of God and of the truths He revealed through the studying of His Word. Encourage your group toward the importance of the application journey and how transformation comes when we not only study the Word of God but act upon what He teaches us.

>**Day 2.** Luke 1:26-38

Leader Notes

Focal Points: (a.) Gabriel's visit to Mary, announcing the coming of Jesus. (b.) Mary's circumstances at the time of Gabriel's visit (engaged/virgin). (c.) The favor of God on Mary's life. (d.) Gabriel's message of the greatness of Jesus. (e.) The reward of Mary's heart of belief. Nothing is too difficult for God. (g.) Mary's obedience to the Word of God.

Revelation: Within the passages studied, ask the ladies to discuss the following: (a.) truths revealed about God's character, (b.) truths revealed that both ministered and encouraged their hearts, (c.) truths that brought conviction of sin and or need of change, (d.) truths revealing God's promises, (e.) truths revealed that restored hope.

Application: Foster to the ladies the importance of applying what they learned of the character of God and of the truths He revealed through the studying of His Word. Encourage your group toward the importance of the application journey and how transformation comes when we not only study the Word of God but act upon what He teaches us.

>**Day 3.** Luke 1:39-56

Leader Notes

Focal Points: (a.) The divine meeting between Elizabeth and Mary. (b.) Lessons gleaned from the ways Elizabeth ministered to Mary and of her recognition of the hand of God upon Mary's life. (c.) Mary's exultation of the Lord's goodness, power, and help toward His people.

Revelation: Within the passages studied, ask the ladies to discuss the following: (a.) truths revealed about God's character, (b.) truths revealed that both ministered and encouraged their hearts, (c.) truths that brought conviction of sin and or need of change, (d.) truths revealing God's promises, (e.) truths revealed that restored hope.

Application: Foster to the ladies the importance of applying what they learned of the character of God and of the truths He revealed through the studying of His Word. Encourage your group toward the importance of the application journey and how transformation comes when we not only study the Word of God but act upon what He teaches us.

>**Day 4.** Luke 1:57-80

Leader Notes

Focal Points: (a.) Elizabeth gives birth. (b.) Zacharias and Elizabeth reveal the child's name is to be John. (d.) Zacharias' voice is restored. (e.) The prophecy of Zacharias regarding John and how he will be used by the Lord. (f.) John's continued growth in the spirit, dwelling in the desert until he appeared publicly to Israel.

Revelation: Within the passages studied, ask the ladies to discuss the following: (a.) truths revealed about God's character, (b.) truths revealed that both ministered and encouraged their hearts, (c.) truths that brought conviction of sin and or need of change, (d.) truths revealing God's promises, (e.) truths revealed that restored hope.

Application: Foster to the ladies the importance of applying what they learned of the character of God and of the truths He revealed through the studying of His Word. Encourage your group toward the importance of the application journey and how transformation comes when we not only study the Word of God but act upon what He teaches us.

>**Day 5.** Feast on God's Truth:
   a. Write out this week's scripture verse.
   b. In what ways does this passage encourage your heart? How can you apply it to your life?

Looking Back at Truths Revealed: Spend time looking back over truths revealed for days 1–4. List below the truth that has resonated the most in your heart this week. (You can list more if you desire.)

Pass It On: Share the lessons you learned this week with your kids, your family, your friends, and those to whom God places in your path. Entrust to others what has been entrusted to you.

Notes

Week 2

Scripture Memory
And Jesus kept increasing in wisdom and stature, and in favor with God and men. (Luke 2:52)

Prayer
Lord Jesus, I come before you during this time of study, asking You to open my heart to hear Your Word and obey Your truth. In Jesus' name I pray, amen.

Scripture Reading By Day
*Truth Revealed: What truths did God reveal to you through today's scripture reading? What did God say to you—to your heart—as you read today's scripture?

*Truth Applied: How will you use what God revealed to you today in your daily life?

>**Day 1.** Luke 2:1-14

Leader Notes

Focal Points: (a.) Mary gives birth to Jesus. (b.) The circumstances surrounding His birth and the scene where He was born. (c.) The angel's message to the shepherds: "For today in the city of David there has been born for you a Savior, who is Christ the Lord." (d.) Jesus was born for you, for me, for everyone. (e.) The multitude of the heavenly host. (f.) What the birth of Jesus means to the world.

Revelation: Within the passages studied, ask the ladies to discuss the following: (a.) truths revealed about God's character, (b.) truths revealed that both ministered and encouraged their hearts, (c.) truths that brought conviction of sin and or need of change, (d.) truths revealing God's promises, (e.) truths revealed that restored hope.

Application: Foster to the ladies the importance of applying what they learned of the character of God and of the truths He revealed through the studying of His Word. Encourage your group toward the importance of the application journey and how transformation comes when we not only study the Word of God but act upon what He teaches us.

>**Day 2.** Luke 2:15-20

Leader Notes

Focal Points: (a.) The shepherds' visit to Jesus. (b.) Shepherds make known what had been told to them about Jesus. (c.) Mary treasured what she heard and pondered over it in her heart. (d.) Shepherds glorify and praise God for what they had seen and heard.

Revelation: Within the passages studied, ask the ladies to discuss the following: (a.) truths revealed about God's character, (b.) truths revealed that both ministered and encouraged their hearts, (c.) truths that brought conviction of sin and or need of change, (d.) truths revealing God's promises, (e.) truths revealed that restored hope.

Application: Foster to the ladies the importance of applying what they learned of the character of God and of the truths He revealed through the studying of His Word. Encourage your group toward the importance of the application journey and how transformation comes when we not only study the Word of God but act upon what He teaches us.

>**Day 3.** Luke 2:21-40

Leader Notes

Focal Points: (a.) His name. (b.) A promise fulfilled to Simeon. (c.) Take note of Simeon's message regarding Jesus in vss. 30-32, 34-35. (d.) The dedication of Anna's life in prayer to God. (e.) Notice vs. 40: God's work in the life of Jesus.

Revelation: Within the passages studied, ask the ladies to discuss the following: (a.) truths revealed about God's character, (b.) truths revealed that both ministered and encouraged their hearts, (c.) truths that brought conviction of sin and or need of change, (d.) truths revealing God's promises, (e.) truths revealed that restored hope.

Application: Foster to the ladies the importance of applying what they learned of the character of God and of the truths He revealed through the studying of His Word. Encourage your group toward the importance of the application journey and how transformation comes when we not only study the Word of God but act upon what He teaches us.

>**Day 4.** Luke 2:41-52

Leader Notes

Focal Points: (a.) After missing for three days, Jesus is found sitting in the temple amid the teachers, both listening to and asking them questions. (b.) People were amazed at the answers given by Jesus and by His understanding. (c.) The question posed to Jesus by His parents (regarding His absence from them) and the response given by Jesus regarding their concern. (d.) Mary treasures "all these things" in her heart. (e.) Areas that Jesus kept increasing in: wisdom, stature, and favor with both God and men.

Revelation: Within the passages studied, ask the ladies to discuss the following: (a.) truths revealed about God's character, (b.) truths revealed that both ministered and encouraged their hearts, (c.) truths that brought conviction of sin and or need of change, (d.) truths revealing God's promises, (e.) truths revealed that restored hope.

Application: Foster to the ladies the importance of applying what they learned of the character of God and of the truths He revealed through the studying of His Word. Encourage your group toward the importance of the application journey and how transformation comes when we not only study the Word of God but act upon what He teaches us.

>**Day 5.** Feast on God's Truth:
   a.   Write out this week's scripture verse.
   b.   In what ways does this passage encourage your heart? How can you apply it to your life?

Looking Back at Truths Revealed: Spend time looking back over truths revealed for days 1–4. List below the truth that has resonated the most in your heart this week. (You can list more if you desire.)

Pass It On: Share the lessons you learned this week with your kids, your family, your friends, and those to whom God places in your path. Entrust to others what has been entrusted to you.

Notes

Week 3

Scripture Memory

Now when all the people were baptized, Jesus was also baptized, and while He was praying, heaven was opened. (Luke 3:21)

Prayer

Lord Jesus, I come before you during this time of study, asking You to open my heart to hear Your Word and obey Your truth. In Jesus' name I pray, amen.

Scripture Reading By Day

***Truth Revealed:** What truths did God reveal to you through today's scripture reading? What did God say to you—to your heart—as you read today's scripture?

***Truth Applied:** How will you use what God revealed to you today in your daily life?

>**Day 1.** Luke 3:1-6

Leader Notes

Focal Points: (a.) The Word of God came to John in the wilderness. (The Lord brought forth John's calling at His appointed time). (b.) John preached a baptism of repentance—prophecy fulfilled. (Note the words spoken by Isaiah the prophet in Luke 3:4-6 as well as by Zacharias in Luke 1).

Revelation: Within the passages studied, ask the ladies to discuss the following: (a.) truths revealed about God's character, (b.) truths revealed that both ministered and encouraged their hearts, (c.) truths that brought conviction of sin and or need of change, (d.) truths revealing God's promises, (e.) truths revealed that restored hope.

Application: Foster to the ladies the importance of applying what they learned of the character of God and of the truths He revealed through the studying of His Word. Encourage your group toward the importance of the application journey and how transformation comes when we not only study the Word of God but act upon what He teaches us.

>**Day 2.** Luke 3:7-20

Leader Notes

Focal Points: (a.) John's message in verse 8: "Bear fruits in keeping with repentance." (b.) John speaks of heart change/what repentance looks like. (c.) John speaks of One coming mightier than he. (d.) The imprisonment of John.

Revelation: Within the passages studied, ask the ladies to discuss the following: (a.) truths revealed about God's character, (b.) truths revealed that both ministered and encouraged their hearts, (c.) truths that brought conviction of sin and or need of change, (d.) truths revealing God's promises, (e.) truths revealed that restored hope.

Application: Foster to the ladies the importance of applying what they learned of the character of God and of the truths He revealed through the studying of His Word. Encourage your group toward the importance of the application journey and how transformation comes when we not only study the Word of God but act upon what He teaches us.

>**Day 3.** Luke 3:21-22

Leader Notes

Focal Points: (a.) The baptism of Jesus. (b.) Jesus prays, heaven opens. (c.) The Holy Spirit descends upon Jesus. (d.) The message from God to Jesus.

Revelation: Within the passages studied, ask the ladies to discuss the following: (a.) truths revealed about God's character, (b.) truths revealed that both ministered and encouraged their hearts, (c.) truths that brought conviction of sin and or need of change, (d.) truths revealing God's promises, (e.) truths revealed that restored hope.

Application: Foster to the ladies the importance of applying what they learned of the character of God and of the truths He revealed through the studying of His Word. Encourage your group toward the importance of the application journey and how transformation comes when we not only study the Word of God but act upon what He teaches us.

>**Day 4.** Luke 3:23-38

Leader Notes

Focal Points: (a.) Jesus begins His ministry at the age of 30. (b.) The lineage (don't miss the importance of the lineage of Jesus).

Revelation: Within the passages studied, ask the ladies to discuss the following: (a.) truths revealed about God's character, (b.) truths revealed that both ministered and encouraged their hearts, (c.) truths that brought conviction of sin and or need of change, (d.) truths revealing God's promises, (e.) truths revealed that restored hope.

Application: Foster to the ladies the importance of applying what they learned of the character of God and of the truths He revealed through the studying of His Word. Encourage your group toward the importance of the application journey and how transformation comes when we not only study the Word of God but act upon what He teaches us.

>**Day 5.** Feast on God's Truth:

a.   Write out this week's scripture verse.

b.   In what ways does this passage encourage your heart? How can you apply it to your life?

Looking Back at Truths Revealed: Spend time looking back over truths revealed for days 1–4. List below the truth that has resonated the most in your heart this week. (You can list more if you desire.)

Pass It On: Share the lessons you learned this week with your kids, your family, your friends, and those to whom God places in your path. Entrust to others what has been entrusted to you.

Notes

Week 4

Scripture Memory

Jesus answered him, "It is written, 'You shall worship the Lord your God and serve Him only.'" (Luke 4:8)

Prayer

Lord Jesus, I come before you during this time of study, asking You to open my heart to hear Your Word and obey Your truth. In Jesus' name I pray, amen.

Scripture Reading By Day

Truth Revealed: What truths did God reveal to you through today's scripture reading? What did God say to you—to your heart—as you read today's scripture?

Truth Applied: How will you use what God revealed to you today in your daily life?

>**Day 1.** Luke 4:1-13

Leader Notes

Focal Points: (a.) Jesus was led by the Spirit into the wilderness to be tempted for 40 days. (b.) What is the significance of 40 days? (c.) What the enemy offered Jesus. (d.) Jesus responds to the devil's temptation according to scripture. (e.) The devil leaves Jesus until the opportune time.

Revelation: Within the passages studied, ask the ladies to discuss the following: (a.) truths revealed about God's character, (b.) truths revealed that both ministered and encouraged their hearts, (c.) truths that brought conviction of sin and or need of change, (d.) truths revealing God's promises, (e.) truths revealed that restored hope.

Application: Foster to the ladies the importance of applying what they learned of the character of God and of the truths He revealed through the studying of His Word. Encourage your group toward the importance of the application journey and how transformation comes when we not only study the Word of God but act upon what He teaches us.

>**Day 2.** Luke 4:14-30

Leader Notes

Focal Points: (a.) Jesus proclaims Himself as Messiah; scripture is fulfilled. (b.) Prophet in His hometown. (c.) Why the people were so angry over the message of Jesus. (d.) The people drive Jesus out of the city. (e.) Where Jesus was led to and the intentions of the people. (f.) Jesus passes through their midst—goes His way.

Revelation: Within the passages studied, ask the ladies to discuss the following: (a.) truths revealed about God's character, (b.) truths revealed that both ministered and encouraged their hearts, (c.) truths that brought conviction of sin and or need of change, (d.) truths revealing God's promises, (e.) truths revealed that restored hope.

Application: Foster to the ladies the importance of applying what they learned of the character of God and of the truths He revealed through the studying of His Word. Encourage your group toward the importance of the application journey and how transformation comes when we not only study the Word of God but act upon what He teaches us.

>Day 3. Luke 4:31-37

Leader Notes

Focal Points: (a.) People amazed at the teaching of Jesus. (b.) The message of Jesus was with authority. (c.) The demon knows who Jesus is. (d.) Jesus intervenes, rebuking and commanding the demon to come out of the man. (e.) The people notice that with "authority" and "power" Jesus commands unclean spirits, and they come out.

Revelation: Within the passages studied, ask the ladies to discuss the following: (a.) truths revealed about God's character, (b.) truths revealed that both ministered and encouraged their hearts, (c.) truths that brought conviction of sin and or need of change, (d.) truths revealing God's promises, (e.) truths revealed that restored hope.

Application: Foster to the ladies the importance of applying what they learned of the character of God and of the truths He revealed through the studying of His Word. Encourage your group toward the importance of the application journey and how transformation comes when we not only study the Word of God but act upon what He teaches us.

>Day 4. Luke 4:38-44

Leader Notes

Focal Points: (a.) Jesus heals. (b.) Demons come out of many, shouting, "You are the Son of God!" (c.) Jesus rebukes the demons, not allowing them to speak. (d.) Jesus knew His purpose.

Revelation: Within the passages studied, ask the ladies to discuss the following: (a.) truths revealed about God's character, (b.) truths revealed that both ministered and encouraged their hearts, (c.) truths that brought conviction of sin and or need of change, (d.) truths revealing God's promises, (e.) truths revealed that restored hope.

Application: Foster to the ladies the importance of applying what they learned of the character of God and of the truths He revealed through the studying of His Word. Encourage your group toward the importance of the application journey and how transformation comes when we not only study the Word of God but act upon what He teaches us.

>Day 5. Feast on God's Truth:

    a.   Write out this week's scripture verse.

    b.   In what ways does this passage encourage your heart? How can you apply it to your life?

Looking Back at Truths Revealed: Spend time looking back over truths revealed for days 1–4. List below the truth that has resonated the most in your heart this week. (You can list more if you desire.)

Pass It On: Share the lessons you learned this week with your kids, your family, your friends, and those to whom God places in your path. Entrust to others what has been entrusted to you.

Notes

Week 5

Scripture Memory

When they had brought their boats to land, they left everything and followed Him. (Luke 5:11)

Prayer

Lord Jesus, I come before you during this time of study, asking You to open my heart to hear Your Word and obey Your truth. In Jesus' name I pray, amen.

Scripture Reading By Day

*Truth Revealed: What truths did God reveal to you through today's scripture reading? What did God say to you—to your heart—as you read today's scripture?

*Truth Applied: How will you use what God revealed to you today in your daily life?

>**Day 1.** Luke 5:1-11

Leader Notes

Focal Points: (a.) Jesus notices two boats and the fishermen who had gotten out and were washing their nets. (b.) Jesus gets into Simon's boat and makes three requests: one, "Pull out a little way from the land"; two, "Put out into the deep water"; three, "Let down your nets for a catch." (c.) Peter obeys all three requests. (d.) The great catch of fish. (e.) Amazement ceases Peter and all his companions. (f.) The message Jesus spoke to Peter as related to fear/catching men. (g.) They left everything and followed Jesus after they brought their boats to land.

Revelation: Within the passages studied, ask the ladies to discuss the following: (a.) truths revealed about God's character, (b.) truths revealed that both ministered and encouraged their hearts, (c.) truths that brought conviction of sin and or need of change, (d.) truths revealing God's promises, (e.) truths revealed that restored hope.

Application: Foster to the ladies the importance of applying what they learned of the character of God and of the truths He revealed through the studying of His Word. Encourage your group toward the importance of the application journey and how transformation comes when we not only study the Word of God but act upon what He teaches us.

>**Day 2.** Luke 5:12-16

Leader Notes

Focal Points: (a.) The declaration spoken to Jesus from the man who had leprosy. (b.) The response of Jesus to the leper. (c.) The healing of leprosy. (d.) Jesus' instructions to the man after the healing took place. (e.) Large crowds gathered to hear Jesus and be healed. (f.) Jesus knew the importance of prayer.

Revelation: Within the passages studied, ask the ladies to discuss the following: (a.) truths revealed about God's character, (b.) truths revealed that both ministered and encouraged their hearts, (c.) truths that brought conviction of sin and or need of change, (d.) truths revealing God's promises, (e.) truths revealed that restored hope.

Application: Foster to the ladies the importance of applying what they learned of the character of God and of the truths He revealed through the studying of His Word. Encourage your group toward the importance of the application journey and how transformation comes when we not only study the Word of God but act upon what He teaches us.

>**Day 3.** Luke 5:17-26

Leader Notes

Focal Points: (a.) The persistence of friends in bringing the paralyzed man to Jesus. (b.) The response of Jesus to their faith. (c.) The reaction of the scribes and Pharisees to the words spoken by Jesus. (d.) The answer given by Jesus in response to the scribes' and Pharisees' reasoning. (e.) Jesus speaks to the paralytic: "Get up, and pick up your stretcher and go home." (f.) The action steps taken by the man who had been paralyzed. (g.) How others were impacted by the miracle performed by Jesus.

Revelation: Within the passages studied, ask the ladies to discuss the following: (a.) truths revealed about God's character, (b.) truths revealed that both ministered and encouraged their hearts, (c.) truths that brought conviction of sin and or need of change, (d.) truths revealing God's promises, (e.) truths revealed that restored hope.

Application: Foster to the ladies the importance of applying what they learned of the character of God and of the truths He revealed through the studying of His Word. Encourage your group toward the importance of the application journey and how transformation comes when we not only study the Word of God but act upon what He teaches us.

>**Day 4.** Luke 5:27-39

Leader Notes

Focal Points: (a.) Jesus notices a tax collector and asks him to follow Him. (b.) Action steps taken by the tax collector in response to the call of Jesus. (c.) Levi's reception and those reclining at the table/the grumblings of the Pharisees and the scribes regarding such a guest. (d.) The response to their grumblings by Jesus. (e.) Jesus challenges the Pharisees with His teaching on the old and new covenant.

Revelation: Within the passages studied, ask the ladies to discuss the following: (a.) truths revealed about God's character, (b.) truths revealed that both ministered and encouraged their hearts, (c.) truths that brought conviction of sin and or need of change, (d.) truths revealing God's promises, (e.) truths revealed that restored hope.

Application: Foster to the ladies the importance of applying what they learned of the character of God and of the truths He revealed through the studying of His Word. Encourage your group toward the importance of the application journey and how transformation comes when we not only study the Word of God but act upon what He teaches us.

>**Day 5.** Feast on God's Truth:

   a. Write out this week's scripture verse.
   b. In what ways does this passage encourage your heart? How can you apply it to your life?

Looking Back at Truths Revealed: Spend time looking back over truths revealed for days 1–4. List below the truth that has resonated the most in your heart this week. (You can list more if you desire.)

Pass It On: Share the lessons you learned this week with your kids, your family, your friends, and those to whom God places in your path. Entrust to others what has been entrusted to you.

Notes

Week 6

Scripture Memory
> *"Treat others the same way you want them to treat you." (Luke 6:31)*

Prayer
Lord Jesus, I come before you during this time of study, asking You to open my heart to hear Your Word and obey Your truth. In Jesus' name I pray, amen.

Scripture Reading By Day
> **Truth Revealed: What truths did God reveal to you through today's scripture reading? What did God say to you—to your heart—as you read today's scripture?*

> **Truth Applied: How will you use what God revealed to you today in your daily life?*

>**Day 1.** Luke 6:1-19

Leader Notes

Focal Points: (a.) The Son of Man, Lord of the Sabbath. (b.) People's response to the Lord's actions carried out on the Sabbath. (c.) Jesus chooses the twelve.

Revelation: Within the passages studied, ask the ladies to discuss the following: (a.) truths revealed about God's character, (b.) truths revealed that both ministered and encouraged their hearts, (c.) truths that brought conviction of sin and or need of change, (d.) truths revealing God's promises, (e.) truths revealed that restored hope.

Application: Foster to the ladies the importance of applying what they learned of the character of God and of the truths He revealed through the studying of His Word. Encourage your group toward the importance of the application journey and how transformation comes when we not only study the Word of God but act upon what He teaches us.

>**Day 2.** Luke 6:20-38

Leader Notes

Focal Points: (a.) The Beatitudes. (b.) Guidelines for kingdom living.

Revelation: Within the passages studied, ask the ladies to discuss the following: (a.) truths revealed about God's character, (b.) truths revealed that both ministered and encouraged their hearts, (c.) truths that brought conviction of sin and or need of change, (d.) truths revealing God's promises, (e.) truths revealed that restored hope.

Application: Foster to the ladies the importance of applying what they learned of the character of God and of the truths He revealed through the studying of His Word. Encourage your group toward the importance of the application journey and how transformation comes when we not only study the Word of God but act upon what He teaches us.

Notes

>**Day 3.** Luke 6:39-45

Leader Notes

Focal Points: (a.) Blind leading the blind. (b.) Logs/specks. (c.) Known by our fruit. (d.) The mouth will speak from that which fills the heart.

Revelation: Within the passages studied, ask the ladies to discuss the following: (a.) truths revealed about God's character, (b.) truths revealed that both ministered and encouraged their hearts, (c.) truths that brought conviction of sin and or need of change, (d.) truths revealing God's promises, (e.) truths revealed that restored hope.

Application: Foster to the ladies the importance of applying what they learned of the character of God and of the truths He revealed through the studying of His Word. Encourage your group toward the importance of the application journey and how transformation comes when we not only study the Word of God but act upon what He teaches us.

>**Day 4.** Luke 6:46-49

Leader Notes

Focal Points: (a.) The importance of building on a solid foundation. (b.) Hearing and acting upon the Word of God.

Revelation: Within the passages studied, ask the ladies to discuss the following: (a.) truths revealed about God's character, (b.) truths revealed that both ministered and encouraged their hearts, (c.) truths that brought conviction of sin and or need of change, (d.) truths revealing God's promises, (e.) truths revealed that restored hope.

Application: Foster to the ladies the importance of applying what they learned of the character of God and of the truths He revealed through the studying of His Word. Encourage your group toward the importance of the application journey and how transformation comes when we not only study the Word of God but act upon what He teaches us.

>**Day 5.** Feast on God's Truth:
  a.   Write out this week's scripture verse.
  b.   In what ways does this passage encourage your heart? How can you apply it to your life?

Looking Back at Truths Revealed: Spend time looking back over truths revealed for days 1–4. List below the truth that has resonated the most in your heart this week. (You can list more if you desire.)

Pass It On: Share the lessons you learned this week with your kids, your family, your friends, and those to whom God places in your path. Entrust to others what has been entrusted to you.

Notes

Week 7

Scripture Memory

And He said to the woman, "Your faith has saved you; go in peace." (Luke 7:50)

Prayer

Lord Jesus, I come before you during this time of study, asking You to open my heart to hear Your Word and obey Your truth. In Jesus' name I pray, amen.

Scripture Reading By Day

__Truth Revealed:__ What truths did God reveal to you through today's scripture reading? What did God say to you—to your heart—as you read today's scripture?

__Truth Applied:__ How will you use what God revealed to you today in your daily life?

>**Day 1.** Luke 7:1-10

Leader Notes

Focal Points: (a.) The Centurion's request to Jesus. (b.) The Centurion's great faith/recognized by Jesus.

Revelation: Within the passages studied, ask the ladies to discuss the following: (a.) truths revealed about God's character, (b.) truths revealed that both ministered and encouraged their hearts, (c.) truths that brought conviction of sin and or need of change, (d.) truths revealing God's promises, (e.) truths revealed that restored hope.

Application: Foster to the ladies the importance of applying what they learned of the character of God and of the truths He revealed through the studying of His Word. Encourage your group toward the importance of the application journey and how transformation comes when we not only study the Word of God but act upon what He teaches us.

>**Day 2.** Luke 7:11-17

Leader Notes

Focal Points: (a.) The death of a son. (b.) The compassion of Jesus. (c.) Giving back the son to his mother. (d.) The impact on and the response of the people after the miracle.

Revelation: Within the passages studied, ask the ladies to discuss the following: (a.) truths revealed about God's character, (b.) truths revealed that both ministered and encouraged their hearts, (c.) truths that brought conviction of sin and or need of change, (d.) truths revealing God's promises, (e.) truths revealed that restored hope.

Application: Foster to the ladies the importance of applying what they learned of the character of God and of the truths He revealed through the studying of His Word. Encourage your group toward the importance of the application journey and how transformation comes when we not only study the Word of God but act upon what He teaches us.

>Day 3. Luke 7:18-35

Leader Notes

Focal Points: (a.) John questions if Jesus is the expected One. (b.) Jesus responds, "Go and report to John what you have seen and heard" (Isaiah 35:5-6, 61:1). (c.) Jesus acknowledges John. (d.) Jesus rebukes the Pharisees.

Revelation: Within the passages studied, ask the ladies to discuss the following: (a.) truths revealed about God's character, (b.) truths revealed that both ministered and encouraged their hearts, (c.) truths that brought conviction of sin and or need of change, (d.) truths revealing God's promises, (e.) truths revealed that restored hope.

Application: Foster to the ladies the importance of applying what they learned of the character of God and of the truths He revealed through the studying of His Word. Encourage your group toward the importance of the application journey and how transformation comes when we not only study the Word of God but act upon what He teaches us.

>Day 4. Luke 7:36-50

Leader Notes

Focal Points: (a.) The encounter between the woman and Jesus at the home of Simon. (b.) The significance of the woman's actions toward Jesus. (c.) The Pharisee's response regarding the actions of the woman. (d.) Jesus' response to the Pharisee. (e.) The message of Jesus to the woman.

Revelation: Within the passages studied, ask the ladies to discuss the following: (a.) truths revealed about God's character, (b.) truths revealed that both ministered and encouraged their hearts, (c.) truths that brought conviction of sin and or need of change, (d.) truths revealing God's promises, (e.) truths revealed that restored hope.

Application: Foster to the ladies the importance of applying what they learned of the character of God and of the truths He revealed through the studying of His Word. Encourage your group toward the importance of the application journey and how transformation comes when we not only study the Word of God but act upon what He teaches us.

>Day 5. Feast on God's Truth:

a. Write out this week's scripture verse.
b. In what ways does this passage encourage your heart? How can you apply it to your life?

Looking Back at Truths Revealed: Spend time looking back over truths revealed for days 1–4. List below the truth that has resonated the most in your heart this week. (You can list more if you desire.)

Pass It On: Share the lessons you learned this week with your kids, your family, your friends, and those to whom God places in your path. Entrust to others what has been entrusted to you.

Week 8

Scripture Memory

They came to Jesus and woke Him up, saying, "Master, Master, we are perishing!" And He got up and rebuked the wind and the surging waves, and they stopped, and it became calm. (Luke 8:24)

Prayer

Lord Jesus, I come before you during this time of study, asking You to open my heart to hear Your Word and obey Your truth. In Jesus' name I pray, amen.

Scripture Reading By Day

*Truth Revealed: What truths did God reveal to you through today's scripture reading? What did God say to you—to your heart—as you read today's scripture?

*Truth Applied: How will you use what God revealed to you today in your daily life?

>**Day 1.** Luke 8:1-21

Leader Notes

Focal Points: (a.) Jesus continues to preach the kingdom of God. (b.) Parables of the sower/lamp. (c) The response of Jesus after learning that His mother and brothers were trying to see Him.

Revelation: Within the passages studied, ask the ladies to discuss the following: (a.) truths revealed about God's character, (b.) truths revealed that both ministered and encouraged their hearts, (c.) truths that brought conviction of sin and or need of change, (d.) truths revealing God's promises, (e.) truths revealed that restored hope.

Application: Foster to the ladies the importance of applying what they learned of the character of God and of the truths He revealed through the studying of His Word. Encourage your group toward the importance of the application journey and how transformation comes when we not only study the Word of God but act upon what He teaches us.

>**Day 2.** Luke 8:22-25

Leader Notes

Focal Points: (a.) The instructions Jesus gave the disciples. (b.) The circumstances that challenged the word He gave to the disciples: "Let us go over to the other side." (c.) Jesus calms the sea and speaks to the disciples. (d.) The disciples' reaction to the miracle Jesus performed.

Revelation: Within the passages studied, ask the ladies to discuss the following: (a.) truths revealed about God's character, (b.) truths revealed that both ministered and encouraged their hearts, (c.) truths that brought conviction of sin and or need of change, (d.) truths revealing God's promises, (e.) truths revealed that restored hope.

Application: Foster to the ladies the importance of applying what they learned of the character of God and of the truths He revealed through the studying of His Word. Encourage your group toward the importance of the application journey and how transformation comes when we not only study the Word of God but act upon what He teaches us.

>Day 3. Luke 8:26-39

Notes

Leader Notes

Focal Points: (a.) The meeting between Jesus and the man possessed by demons. (b.) Jesus frees the man of demon possession. (c.) The state by which the people find the man after he has been healed. (d.) The mission issued by Jesus to the man healed.

Revelation: Within the passages studied, ask the ladies to discuss the following: (a.) truths revealed about God's character, (b.) truths revealed that both ministered and encouraged their hearts, (c.) truths that brought conviction of sin and or need of change, (d.) truths revealing God's promises, (e.) truths revealed that restored hope.

Application: Foster to the ladies the importance of applying what they learned of the character of God and of the truths He revealed through the studying of His Word. Encourage your group toward the importance of the application journey and how transformation comes when we not only study the Word of God but act upon what He teaches us.

>Day 4. Luke 8:40-56

Leader Notes

Focal Points: (a.) The petition of Jairus to Jesus. (b.) The woman with the issue of blood. (c.) The message from Jesus to the woman. (d.) The message about Jairus's daughter and the response of Jesus. (e.) The miracle brought forth by Jesus.

Revelation: Within the passages studied, ask the ladies to discuss the following: (a.) truths revealed about God's character, (b.) truths revealed that both ministered and encouraged their hearts, (c.) truths that brought conviction of sin and or need of change, (d.) truths revealing God's promises, (e.) truths revealed that restored hope.

Application: Foster to the ladies the importance of applying what they learned of the character of God and of the truths He revealed through the studying of His Word. Encourage your group toward the importance of the application journey and how transformation comes when we not only study the Word of God but act upon what He teaches us.

>Day 5. Feast on God's Truth:

a. Write out this week's scripture verse.

b. In what ways does this passage encourage your heart? How can you apply it to your life?

Looking Back at Truths Revealed: Spend time looking back over truths revealed for days 1–4. List below the truth that has resonated the most in your heart this week. (You can list more if you desire.)

Pass It On: Share the lessons you learned this week with your kids, your family, your friends, and those to whom God places in your path. Entrust to others what has been entrusted to you.

Notes

Week 9

Scripture Memory
". . . for the Son of Man did not come to destroy men's lives, but to save them." And they went on to another village. (Luke 9:56)

Prayer
Lord Jesus, I come before you during this time of study, asking You to open my heart to hear Your Word and obey Your truth. In Jesus' name I pray, amen.

SCRIPTURE READING BY DAY

***Truth Revealed:** What truths did God reveal to you through today's scripture reading? What did God say to you—to your heart—as you read today's scripture?*

***Truth Applied:** How will you use what God revealed to you today in your daily life?*

>**Day 1.** Luke 9:1-17

Leader Notes

Focal Points: (a.) Jesus sends out the twelve. (b.) The feeding of the five thousand; the need, the scene, the miracle.

Revelation: Within the passages studied, ask the ladies to discuss the following: (a.) truths revealed about God's character, (b.) truths revealed that both ministered and encouraged their hearts, (c.) truths that brought conviction of sin and or need of change, (d.) truths revealing God's promises, (e.) truths revealed that restored hope.

Application: Foster to the ladies the importance of applying what they learned of the character of God and of the truths He revealed through the studying of His Word. Encourage your group toward the importance of the application journey and how transformation comes when we not only study the Word of God but act upon what He teaches us.

>**Day 2.** Luke 9:18-27

Leader Notes

Focal Points: (a.) The question posed by Jesus, "But who do you say that I am?" (b.) Peter's response to the question. (c.) Jesus taught, "If anyone wants to come after Me, he must deny himself, take up his cross daily, and follow Me."

Revelation: Within the passages studied, ask the ladies to discuss the following: (a.) truths revealed about God's character, (b.) truths revealed that both ministered and encouraged their hearts, (c.) truths that brought conviction of sin and or need of change, (d.) truths revealing God's promises, (e.) truths revealed that restored hope.

Application: Foster to the ladies the importance of applying what they learned of the character of God and of the truths He revealed through the studying of His Word. Encourage your group toward the importance of the application journey and how transformation comes when we not only study the Word of God but act upon what He teaches us.

>Day 3. Luke 9:28-45

Leader Notes

Focal Points: (a.) The Transfiguration, His glory, His upcoming death, and the significance of the Lord telling those to listen to His Son. (b.) Jesus rebukes the unclean spirit, heals the son, and gives him back to his father. (c.) People were amazed at the greatness of God. (d.) Jesus prepares His disciples for what is to come.

Revelation: Within the passages studied, ask the ladies to discuss the following: (a.) truths revealed about God's character, (b.) truths revealed that both ministered and encouraged their hearts, (c.) truths that brought conviction of sin and or need of change, (d.) truths revealing God's promises, (e.) truths revealed that restored hope.

Application: Foster to the ladies the importance of applying what they learned of the character of God and of the truths He revealed through the studying of His Word. Encourage your group toward the importance of the application journey and how transformation comes when we not only study the Word of God but act upon what He teaches us.

>Day 4. Luke 9:46-62

Leader Notes

Focal Points: (a.) The argument about who is the greatest; the answer from Jesus. (b.) Jesus rebukes James and John. (c.) Following Jesus: putting our hands to the plow and not looking back.

Revelation: Within the passages studied, ask the ladies to discuss the following: (a.) truths revealed about God's character, (b.) truths revealed that both ministered and encouraged their hearts, (c.) truths that brought conviction of sin and or need of change, (d.) truths revealing God's promises, (e.) truths revealed that restored hope.

Application: Foster to the ladies the importance of applying what they learned of the character of God and of the truths He revealed through the studying of His Word. Encourage your group toward the importance of the application journey and how transformation comes when we not only study the Word of God but act upon what He teaches us.

>Day 5. Feast on God's Truth:

a.   Write out this week's scripture verse.

b.   In what ways does this passage encourage your heart? How can you apply it to your life?

Looking Back at Truths Revealed: Spend time looking back over truths revealed for days 1–4. List below the truth that has resonated the most in your heart this week. (You can list more if you desire.)

Pass It On: Share the lessons you learned this week with your kids, your family, your friends, and those to whom God places in your path. Entrust to others what has been entrusted to you.

Notes

Week 10

Scripture Memory
She had a sister called Mary, who was seated at the Lord's feet, listening to His word. (Luke 10:39)

Prayer
Lord Jesus, I come before you during this time of study, asking You to open my heart to hear Your Word and obey Your truth. In Jesus' name I pray, amen.

Scripture Reading By Day
*Truth Revealed: What truths did God reveal to you through today's scripture reading? What did God say to you—to your heart—as you read today's scripture?

*Truth Applied: How will you use what God revealed to you today in your daily life?

>**Day 1.** Luke 10:1-16

Leader Notes

Focal Points: (a.) Jesus sends out laborers. (b.) Jesus states to "Beseech the Lord of the harvest." (c.) Instructions given to those sent out by Jesus. (d.) An important truth and reminder given to those sent out by Jesus in vs. 16.

Revelation: Within the passages studied, ask the ladies to discuss the following: (a.) truths revealed about God's character, (b.) truths revealed that both ministered and encouraged their hearts, (c.) truths that brought conviction of sin and or need of change, (d.) truths revealing God's promises, (e.) truths revealed that restored hope.

Application: Foster to the ladies the importance of applying what they learned of the character of God and of the truths He revealed through the studying of His Word. Encourage your group toward the importance of the application journey and how transformation comes when we not only study the Word of God but act upon what He teaches us.

>**Day 2.** Luke 10:17-24

Leader Notes

Focal Points: (a.) Those sent out return joyfully, sharing the results with Jesus. (b.) The prayer of Jesus to His Father. (c.) The message of Jesus to His disciples.

Revelation: Within the passages studied, ask the ladies to discuss the following: (a.) truths revealed about God's character, (b.) truths revealed that both ministered and encouraged their hearts, (c.) truths that brought conviction of sin and or need of change, (d.) truths revealing God's promises, (e.) truths revealed that restored hope.

Application: Foster to the ladies the importance of applying what they learned of the character of God and of the truths He revealed through the studying of His Word. Encourage your group toward the importance of the application journey and how transformation comes when we not only study the Word of God but act upon what He teaches us.

>**Day 3.** Luke 10:25-37   *Notes*

Leader Notes

Focal Points: (a.) Who is my neighbor? (b.) The Good Samaritan.

Revelation: Within the passages studied, ask the ladies to discuss the following: (a.) truths revealed about God's character, (b.) truths revealed that both ministered and encouraged their hearts, (c.) truths that brought conviction of sin and or need of change, (d.) truths revealing God's promises, (e.) truths revealed that restored hope.

Application: Foster to the ladies the importance of applying what they learned of the character of God and of the truths He revealed through the studying of His Word. Encourage your group toward the importance of the application journey and how transformation comes when we not only study the Word of God but act upon what He teaches us.

>**Day 4.** Luke 10:38-42

Leader Notes

Focal Points: (a.) The heart condition of Mary and lessons learned. (b.) The heart condition of Martha and lessons learned. (c.) Lesson taught by Jesus.

Revelation: Within the passages studied, ask the ladies to discuss the following: (a.) truths revealed about God's character, (b.) truths revealed that both ministered and encouraged their hearts, (c.) truths that brought conviction of sin and or need of change, (d.) truths revealing God's promises, (e.) truths revealed that restored hope.

Application: Foster to the ladies the importance of applying what they learned of the character of God and of the truths He revealed through the studying of His Word. Encourage your group toward the importance of the application journey and how transformation comes when we not only study the Word of God but act upon what He teaches us.

>**Day 5.** Feast on God's Truth:

a. Write out this week's scripture verse.
b. In what ways does this passage encourage your heart? How can you apply it to your life?

Looking Back at Truths Revealed: Spend time looking back over truths revealed for days 1–4. List below the truth that has resonated the most in your heart this week. (You can list more if you desire.)

Pass It On: Share the lessons you learned this week with your kids, your family, your friends, and those to whom God places in your path. Entrust to others what has been entrusted to you.

Notes

Week 11

Scripture Memory
"So I say to you, ask, and it will be given to you; seek, and you will find; knock, and it will be opened to you." (Luke 11:9)

Prayer
Lord Jesus, I come before you during this time of study, asking You to open my heart to hear Your Word and obey Your truth. In Jesus' name I pray, amen.

Scripture Reading By Day

***Truth Revealed:** What truths did God reveal to you through today's scripture reading? What did God say to you—to your heart—as you read today's scripture?*

***Truth Applied:** How will you use what God revealed to you today in your daily life?*

>**Day 1.** Luke 11:1-13

Leader Notes

Focal Points: (a.) The question posed to Jesus about prayer. (b.) The answer given by Jesus. (c.) The examples Jesus gives in teaching on prayer. (d.) The significance of persistence in prayer. (e.) Ask, seek, and knock. (f.) Earthly fathers/Heavenly Father.

Revelation: Within the passages studied, ask the ladies to discuss the following: (a.) truths revealed about God's character, (b.) truths revealed that both ministered and encouraged their hearts, (c.) truths that brought conviction of sin and or need of change, (d.) truths revealing God's promises, (e.) truths revealed that restored hope.

Application: Foster to the ladies the importance of applying what they learned of the character of God and of the truths He revealed through the studying of His Word. Encourage your group toward the importance of the application journey and how transformation comes when we not only study the Word of God but act upon what He teaches us.

>**Day 2.** Luke 11:14-28

Leader Notes

Focal Points: (a.) Jesus cast out a demon. (b.) Some stated that Jesus cast out demons by Beelzebul; others wanted to test Jesus, demanding of Him a sign from heaven. (c.) Jesus knew their thoughts and spoke. (d.) The importance of hearing the word of God and observing it.

Revelation: Within the passages studied, ask the ladies to discuss the following: (a.) truths revealed about God's character, (b.) truths revealed that both ministered and encouraged their hearts, (c.) truths that brought conviction of sin and or need of change, (d.) truths revealing God's promises, (e.) truths revealed that restored hope.

Application: Foster to the ladies the importance of applying what they learned of the character of God and of the truths He revealed through the studying of His Word. Encourage your group toward the importance of the application journey and how transformation comes when we not only study the Word of God but act upon what He teaches us.

>**Day 3.** Luke 11:29-36

Notes

Leader Notes

Focal Points: (a.) Jesus discusses sign seeking and the sign of Jonah. (b.) The lamp and the Word of God. (c.) The eye is the lamp of the body—a problematic perception.

Revelation: Within the passages studied, ask the ladies to discuss the following: (a.) truths revealed about God's character, (b.) truths revealed that both ministered and encouraged their hearts, (c.) truths that brought conviction of sin and or need of change, (d.) truths revealing God's promises, (e.) truths revealed that restored hope.

Application: Foster to the ladies the importance of applying what they learned of the character of God and of the truths He revealed through the studying of His Word. Encourage your group toward the importance of the application journey and how transformation comes when we not only study the Word of God but act upon what He teaches us.

>**Day 4.** Luke 11:37-54

Leader Notes

Focal Points: (a.) The "Woes to you." (b.) The response to the "Woes to you."

Revelation: Within the passages studied, ask the ladies to discuss the following: (a.) truths revealed about God's character, (b.) truths revealed that both ministered and encouraged their hearts, (c.) truths that brought conviction of sin and or need of change, (d.) truths revealing God's promises, (e.) truths revealed that restored hope.

Application: Foster to the ladies the importance of applying what they learned of the character of God and of the truths He revealed through the studying of His Word. Encourage your group toward the importance of the application journey and how transformation comes when we not only study the Word of God but act upon what He teaches us.

>**Day 5.** Feast on God's Truth:

a.   Write out this week's scripture verse.

b.   In what ways does this passage encourage your heart? How can you apply it to your life?

Looking Back at Truths Revealed: Spend time looking back over truths revealed for days 1–4. List below the truth that has resonated the most in your heart this week. (You can list more if you desire.)

Pass It On: Share the lessons you learned this week with your kids, your family, your friends, and those to whom God places in your path. Entrust to others what has been entrusted to you.

Notes

Week 12

Scripture Memory

"Are not five sparrows sold for two cents? Yet not one of them is forgotten before God. Indeed, the very hairs of your head are all numbered. Do not fear; you are more valuable than many sparrows." (Luke 12:6-7)

Prayer

Lord Jesus, I come before you during this time of study, asking You to open my heart to hear Your Word and obey Your truth. In Jesus' name I pray, amen.

Scripture Reading By Day

*Truth Revealed: What truths did God reveal to you through today's scripture reading? What did God say to you—to your heart—as you read today's scripture?

*Truth Applied: How will you use what God revealed to you today in your daily life?

>**Day 1.** Luke 12:1-12

Leader Notes

Focal Points: (a.) Leaven of the Pharisees and hypocrisy. (b.) More valuable than sparrows. (c.) Confessing God before men vs. denying God before men. (d.) Blaspheming against the Holy Spirit. (e.) Jesus encourages against fear when brought before the synagogues, rulers, and authorities—for the Holy Spirit will teach what to say.

Revelation: Within the passages studied, ask the ladies to discuss the following: (a.) truths revealed about God's character, (b.) truths revealed that both ministered and encouraged their hearts, (c.) truths that brought conviction of sin and or need of change, (d.) truths revealing God's promises, (e.) truths revealed that restored hope.

Application: Foster to the ladies the importance of applying what they learned of the character of God and of the truths He revealed through the studying of His Word. Encourage your group toward the importance of the application journey and how transformation comes when we not only study the Word of God but act upon what He teaches us.

>**Day 2.** Luke 12:13-34

Leader Notes

Focal Points: (a.) Covetousness. (b.) Jesus says not to worry. (c.) The significance of seeking first the kingdom of God. (d.) "For where you treasure is, there your heart will be also."

Revelation: Within the passages studied, ask the ladies to discuss the following: (a.) truths revealed about God's character, (b.) truths revealed that both ministered and encouraged their hearts, (c.) truths that brought conviction of sin and or need of change, (d.) truths revealing God's promises, (e.) truths revealed that restored hope.

Application: Foster to the ladies the importance of applying what they learned of the character of God and of the truths He revealed through the studying of His Word. Encourage your group toward the importance of the application journey and how transformation comes when we not only study the Word of God but act upon what He teaches us.

>**Day 3.** Luke 12:35-48

Leader Notes

Focal Points: (a.) The importance of being ready. (b.) The question posed by Peter and the answer given by Jesus.

Revelation: Within the passages studied, ask the ladies to discuss the following: (a.) truths revealed about God's character, (b.) truths revealed that both ministered and encouraged their hearts, (c.) truths that brought conviction of sin and or need of change, (d.) truths revealing God's promises, (e.) truths revealed that restored hope.

Application: Foster to the ladies the importance of applying what they learned of the character of God and of the truths He revealed through the studying of His Word. Encourage your group toward the importance of the application journey and how transformation comes when we not only study the Word of God but act upon what He teaches us.

>**Day 4.** Luke 12:49-59

Leader Notes

Focal Points: (a.) Peace and division. (b.) Jesus discusses discerning the times with examples given.

Revelation: Within the passages studied, ask the ladies to discuss the following: (a.) truths revealed about God's character, (b.) truths revealed that both ministered and encouraged their hearts, (c.) truths that brought conviction of sin and or need of change, (d.) truths revealing God's promises, (e.) truths revealed that restored hope.

Application: Foster to the ladies the importance of applying what they learned of the character of God and of the truths He revealed through the studying of His Word. Encourage your group toward the importance of the application journey and how transformation comes when we not only study the Word of God but act upon what He teaches us.

>**Day 5.** Feast on God's Truth:
   a.   Write out this week's scripture verse.
   b.   In what ways does this passage encourage your heart? How can you apply it to your life?

Looking Back at Truths Revealed: Spend time looking back over truths revealed for days 1–4. List below the truth that has resonated the most in your heart this week. (You can list more if you desire.)

Pass It On: Share the lessons you learned this week with your kids, your family, your friends, and those to whom God places in your path. Entrust to others what has been entrusted to you.

Commitment

As you continue this study, consider the commitment pledge below and its significance to your personal experience through this study.

I commit to the next 12 weeks of *Going Deeper* through engaging in the following: (1) weekly attendance, (2) completion of Bible study/homework, (3) scripture memorization, (4) accountability to my group, (5) praying for members of my group, and (6) confidentiality.

Name: _____

Date: _____

Weeks 13–24

The Gospel of Luke 13–24

Segment 2

Notes

Week 13

Scripture Memory

And He was passing through from one city and village to another, teaching, and proceeding on His way to Jerusalem. (Luke 13:22)

Prayer

Lord Jesus, I come before you during this time of study, asking You to open my heart to hear Your Word and obey Your truth. In Jesus' name I pray, amen.

Scripture Reading By Day

*Truth Revealed: What truths did God reveal to you through today's scripture reading? What did God say to you—to your heart—as you read today's scripture?

*Truth Applied: How will you use what God revealed to you today in your daily life?

>**Day 1.** Luke 13:1-9

Leader Notes

Focal Points: (a.) Repentance, the fig tree, and fruit. (b.) Healing of the woman.

Revelation: Within the passages studied, ask the ladies to discuss the following: (a.) truths revealed about God's character, (b.) truths revealed that both ministered and encouraged their hearts, (c.) truths that brought conviction of sin and or need of change, (d.) truths revealing God's promises, (e.) truths revealed that restored hope.

Application: Foster to the ladies the importance of applying what they learned of the character of God and of the truths He revealed through the studying of His Word. Encourage your group toward the importance of the application journey and how transformation comes when we not only study the Word of God but act upon what He teaches us.

>**Day 2.** Luke 13:10-17

Leader Notes

Focal Points: (a.) Jesus heals the woman. (b.) The Synagogue official indignant about Jesus healing on the Sabbath. (c.) Jesus rebukes the Synagogue official. (d.) Opponents humiliated, crowd rejoiced.

Revelation: Within the passages studied, ask the ladies to discuss the following: (a.) truths revealed about God's character, (b.) truths revealed that both ministered and encouraged their hearts, (c.) truths that brought conviction of sin and or need of change, (d.) truths revealing God's promises, (e.) truths revealed that restored hope.

Application: Foster to the ladies the importance of applying what they learned of the character of God and of the truths He revealed through the studying of His Word. Encourage your group toward the importance of the application journey and how transformation comes when we not only study the Word of God but act upon what He teaches us.

>Day 3. Luke 13:18-30

Leader Notes

Focal Points: (a.) The kingdom of God, mustard seed, and leaven. (b.) As Jesus travels, He teaches. (c.) The message of Jesus: strive to enter through the narrow door; many seek to enter but will not be able—rejected Christ as Messiah.

Revelation: Within the passages studied, ask the ladies to discuss the following: (a.) truths revealed about God's character, (b.) truths revealed that both ministered and encouraged their hearts, (c.) truths that brought conviction of sin and or need of change, (d.) truths revealing God's promises, (e.) truths revealed that restored hope.

Application: Foster to the ladies the importance of applying what they learned of the character of God and of the truths He revealed through the studying of His Word. Encourage your group toward the importance of the application journey and how transformation comes when we not only study the Word of God but act upon what He teaches us.

>Day 4. Luke 13:31-35

Leader Notes

Focal Points: (a.) The Pharisees' message to Jesus. (b.) The response of Jesus. (c.) Oh, Jerusalem, Jerusalem.

Revelation: Within the passages studied, ask the ladies to discuss the following: (a.) truths revealed about God's character, (b.) truths revealed that both ministered and encouraged their hearts, (c.) truths that brought conviction of sin and or need of change, (d.) truths revealing God's promises, (e.) truths revealed that restored hope.

Application: Foster to the ladies the importance of applying what they learned of the character of God and of the truths He revealed through the studying of His Word. Encourage your group toward the importance of the application journey and how transformation comes when we not only study the Word of God but act upon what He teaches us.

>Day 5. Feast on God's Truth:
a. Write out this week's scripture verse.
b. In what ways does this passage encourage your heart? How can you apply it to your life?

Looking Back at Truths Revealed: Spend time looking back over truths revealed for days 1–4. List below the truth that has resonated the most in your heart this week. (You can list more if you desire.)

Pass It On: Share the lessons you learned this week with your kids, your family, your friends, and those to whom God places in your path. Entrust to others what has been entrusted to you.

Notes

Week 14

Scripture Memory

"And the master said to the slave, 'Go out into the highways and along the hedges, and compel them to come in, so that my house may be filled.'" (Luke 14:23)

Prayer

Lord Jesus, I come before you during this time of study, asking You to open my heart to hear Your Word and obey Your truth. In Jesus' name I pray, amen.

Scripture Reading By Day

*Truth Revealed: What truths did God reveal to you through today's scripture reading? What did God say to you—to your heart—as you read today's scripture?

*Truth Applied: How will you use what God revealed to you today in your daily life?

>**Day 1.** Luke 14:1-6

Leader Notes

Focal Points: (a.) Jesus enters a house and is watched closely. (b.) The man suffering from dropsy. (c.) Jesus poses a question. (d.) Jesus heals on the Sabbath. (e.) Following the healing, Jesus poses a question.

Revelation: Within the passages studied, ask the ladies to discuss the following: (a.) truths revealed about God's character, (b.) truths revealed that both ministered and encouraged their hearts, (c.) truths that brought conviction of sin and or need of change, (d.) truths revealing God's promises, (e.) truths revealed that restored hope.

Application: Foster to the ladies the importance of applying what they learned of the character of God and of the truths He revealed through the studying of His Word. Encourage your group toward the importance of the application journey and how transformation comes when we not only study the Word of God but act upon what He teaches us.

>**Day 2.** Luke 14:7-14

Leader Notes

Focal Points: (a.) Self-importance and self-exaltation. (b.) The details of verse 11. (c.) What is true charity? (d.) Living with eternal perspective.

Revelation: Within the passages studied, ask the ladies to discuss the following: (a.) truths revealed about God's character, (b.) truths revealed that both ministered and encouraged their hearts, (c.) truths that brought conviction of sin and or need of change, (d.) truths revealing God's promises, (e.) truths revealed that restored hope.

Application: Foster to the ladies the importance of applying what they learned of the character of God and of the truths He revealed through the studying of His Word. Encourage your group toward the importance of the application journey and how transformation comes when we not only study the Word of God but act upon what He teaches us.

>Day 3. Luke 14:15-24

Leader Notes

Focal Points: (a.) Parable of the dinner: invitation and excuses. (b.) Compel them to come; the house may be filled.

Revelation: Within the passages studied, ask the ladies to discuss the following: (a.) truths revealed about God's character, (b.) truths revealed that both ministered and encouraged their hearts, (c.) truths that brought conviction of sin and or need of change, (d.) truths revealing God's promises, (e.) truths revealed that restored hope.

Application: Foster to the ladies the importance of applying what they learned of the character of God and of the truths He revealed through the studying of His Word. Encourage your group toward the importance of the application journey and how transformation comes when we not only study the Word of God but act upon what He teaches us.

>Day 4. Luke 14:25-35

Leader Notes

Focal Points: (a.) Our allegiance to Christ. (b.) Counting the cost. (c.) Seasonless salt.

Revelation: Within the passages studied, ask the ladies to discuss the following: (a.) truths revealed about God's character, (b.) truths revealed that both ministered and encouraged their hearts, (c.) truths that brought conviction of sin and or need of change, (d.) truths revealing God's promises, (e.) truths revealed that restored hope.

Application: Foster to the ladies the importance of applying what they learned of the character of God and of the truths He revealed through the studying of His Word. Encourage your group toward the importance of the application journey and how transformation comes when we not only study the Word of God but act upon what He teaches us.

>Day 5. Feast on God's Truth:

a.   Write out this week's scripture verse.
b.   In what ways does this passage encourage your heart? How can you apply it to your life?

Looking Back at Truths Revealed: Spend time looking back over truths revealed for days 1–4. List below the truth that has resonated the most in your heart this week. (You can list more if you desire.)

Pass It On: Share the lessons you learned this week with your kids, your family, your friends, and those to whom God places in your path. Entrust to others what has been entrusted to you.

Notes

Week 15

Scripture Memory

"I tell you that in the same way, there will be more joy in heaven over one sinner who repents than over ninety-nine righteous persons who need no repentance." (Luke 15:7)

Prayer

Lord Jesus, I come before you during this time of study, asking You to open my heart to hear Your Word and obey Your truth. In Jesus' name I pray, amen.

Scripture Reading By Day

*Truth Revealed: What truths did God reveal to you through today's scripture reading? What did God say to you—to your heart—as you read today's scripture?

*Truth Applied: How will you use what God revealed to you today in your daily life?

>**Day 1.** Luke 15:1-7

Leader Notes

Focal Points: (a.) The lost sheep. (b.) The search for the sheep. (c.) The rejoicing over the sheep that's found. (d.) Joy in heaven and repentance.

Revelation: Within the passages studied, ask the ladies to discuss the following: (a.) truths revealed about God's character, (b.) truths revealed that both ministered and encouraged their hearts, (c.) truths that brought conviction of sin and or need of change, (d.) truths revealing God's promises, (e.) truths revealed that restored hope.

Application: Foster to the ladies the importance of applying what they learned of the character of God and of the truths He revealed through the studying of His Word. Encourage your group toward the importance of the application journey and how transformation comes when we not only study the Word of God but act upon what He teaches us.

>**Day 2.** Luke 15:8-10

Leader Notes

Focal Points: (a.) The search for coins and what it represents. (b.) Joy over one sinner who repents.

Revelation: Within the passages studied, ask the ladies to discuss the following: (a.) truths revealed about God's character, (b.) truths revealed that both ministered and encouraged their hearts, (c.) truths that brought conviction of sin and or need of change, (d.) truths revealing God's promises, (e.) truths revealed that restored hope.

Application: Foster to the ladies the importance of applying what they learned of the character of God and of the truths He revealed through the studying of His Word. Encourage your group toward the importance of the application journey and how transformation comes when we not only study the Word of God but act upon what He teaches us.

>Day 3. Luke 15:11-24

Leader Notes

Focal Points: (a.) The request from the younger son. (b.) The journey and the estate squandered. (c.) The state of the youngest son after he lost his inheritance. (d.) The decisions made and actions taken by the son: one, he came to his senses and remembered home; two, he got up; three, he came to his father; four, he repented. (e.) The father's response to the son's return: one, he saw the son from a distance coming home; two, he ran to meet him; three, he embraced him and accepted him; four, he celebrated him—a picture of the cross.

Revelation: Within the passages studied, ask the ladies to discuss the following: (a.) truths revealed about God's character, (b.) truths revealed that both ministered and encouraged their hearts, (c.) truths that brought conviction of sin and or need of change, (d.) truths revealing God's promises, (e.) truths revealed that restored hope.

Application: Foster to the ladies the importance of applying what they learned of the character of God and of the truths He revealed through the studying of His Word. Encourage your group toward the importance of the application journey and how transformation comes when we not only study the Word of God but act upon what He teaches us.

>Day 4. Luke 15:25-32

Leader Notes

Focal Points: (a.) The older brother's response to the younger brother's return. (b.) The response of the father to the older son's reaction toward the younger brother's return. (c.) The father's message in verse 32.

Revelation: Within the passages studied, ask the ladies to discuss the following: (a.) truths revealed about God's character, (b.) truths revealed that both ministered and encouraged their hearts, (c.) truths that brought conviction of sin and or need of change, (d.) truths revealing God's promises, (e.) truths revealed that restored hope.

Application: Foster to the ladies the importance of applying what they learned of the character of God and of the truths He revealed through the studying of His Word. Encourage your group toward the importance of the application journey and how transformation comes when we not only study the Word of God but act upon what He teaches us.

>Day 5. Feast on God's Truth:

  a.   Write out this week's scripture verse.
  b.   In what ways does this passage encourage your heart? How can you apply it to your life?

Looking Back at Truths Revealed: Spend time looking back over truths revealed for days 1–4. List below the truth that has resonated the most in your heart this week. (You can list more if you desire.)

Pass It On: Share the lessons you learned this week with your kids, your family, your friends, and those to whom God places in your path. Entrust to others what has been entrusted to you.

Notes

Week 16

Scripture Memory

"No servant can serve two masters; for either he will hate the one and love the other, or else he will be devoted to one and despise the other. You cannot serve God and wealth." (Luke 16:13)

Prayer

Lord Jesus, I come before you during this time of study, asking You to open my heart to hear Your Word and obey Your truth. In Jesus' name I pray, amen.

Scripture Reading By Day

Truth Revealed: What truths did God reveal to you through today's scripture reading? What did God say to you—to your heart—as you read today's scripture?

Truth Applied: How will you use what God revealed to you today in your daily life?

>**Day 1.** Luke 16:1-13

Leader Notes

Focal Points: (a.) Stewardship. (b.) Faithful in the least, faithful in the much. (c.) No servant can serve two masters.

Revelation: Within the passages studied, ask the ladies to discuss the following: (a.) truths revealed about God's character, (b.) truths revealed that both ministered and encouraged their hearts, (c.) truths that brought conviction of sin and or need of change, (d.) truths revealing God's promises, (e.) truths revealed that restored hope.

Application: Foster to the ladies the importance of applying what they learned of the character of God and of the truths He revealed through the studying of His Word. Encourage your group toward the importance of the application journey and how transformation comes when we not only study the Word of God but act upon what He teaches us.

>**Day 2.** Luke 16:13

Leader Notes

Focal Points: (a.) Serving two masters: God and wealth. (b.) Lessons taught.

Revelation: Within the passages studied, ask the ladies to discuss the following: (a.) truths revealed about God's character, (b.) truths revealed that both ministered and encouraged their hearts, (c.) truths that brought conviction of sin and or need of change, (d.) truths revealing God's promises, (e.) truths revealed that restored hope.

Application: Foster to the ladies the importance of applying what they learned of the character of God and of the truths He revealed through the studying of His Word. Encourage your group toward the importance of the application journey and how transformation comes when we not only study the Word of God but act upon what He teaches us.

>**Day 3.** Luke 16:14-18   *Notes*

Leader Notes

Focal Points: (a.) Pharisees scoffing. (b.) God knows the heart. (c.) The law and the prophets were proclaimed. (d.) Teaching on divorce.

Revelation: Within the passages studied, ask the ladies to discuss the following: (a.) truths revealed about God's character, (b.) truths revealed that both ministered and encouraged their hearts, (c.) truths that brought conviction of sin and or need of change, (d.) truths revealing God's promises, (e.) truths revealed that restored hope.

Application: Foster to the ladies the importance of applying what they learned of the character of God and of the truths He revealed through the studying of His Word. Encourage your group toward the importance of the application journey and how transformation comes when we not only study the Word of God but act upon what He teaches us.

>**Day 4.** Luke 16:19-31

Leader Notes

Focal Points: (a.) The state of the rich man and Lazarus while on earth; the state of the rich man and Lazarus after death. (b.) The dialogue between the rich man and Abraham, the rich man's requests, and Abraham's responses. (c.) Important lessons learned.

Revelation: Within the passages studied, ask the ladies to discuss the following: (a.) truths revealed about God's character, (b.) truths revealed that both ministered and encouraged their hearts, (c.) truths that brought conviction of sin and or need of change, (d.) truths revealing God's promises, (e.) truths revealed that restored hope.

Application: Foster to the ladies the importance of applying what they learned of the character of God and of the truths He revealed through the studying of His Word. Encourage your group toward the importance of the application journey and how transformation comes when we not only study the Word of God but act upon what He teaches us.

>**Day 5.** Feast on God's Truth:

   a.   Write out this week's scripture verse.
   b.   In what ways does this passage encourage your heart? How can you apply it to your life?

Looking Back at Truths Revealed: Spend time looking back over truths revealed for days 1–4. List below the truth that has resonated the most in your heart this week. (You can list more if you desire.)

Pass It On: Share the lessons you learned this week with your kids, your family, your friends, and those to whom God places in your path. Entrust to others what has been entrusted to you.

Notes

Week 17

Scripture Memory
"And if he sins against you seven times a day, and returns to you seven times, saying, 'I repent,' forgive him." (Luke 17:4)

Prayer
Lord Jesus, I come before you during this time of study, asking You to open my heart to hear Your Word and obey Your truth. In Jesus' name I pray, amen.

Scripture Reading By Day
***Truth Revealed:** What truths did God reveal to you through today's scripture reading? What did God say to you—to your heart—as you read today's scripture?*

***Truth Applied:** How will you use what God revealed to you today in your daily life?*

>**Day 1.** Luke 17:1-4

Leader Notes

Focal Points: (a.) Causing others to stumble. (b.) Jesus' instructions for when a brother sins.

Revelation: Within the passages studied, ask the ladies to discuss the following: (a.) truths revealed about God's character, (b.) truths revealed that both ministered and encouraged their hearts, (c.) truths that brought conviction of sin and or need of change, (d.) truths revealing God's promises, (e.) truths revealed that restored hope.

Application: Foster to the ladies the importance of applying what they learned of the character of God and of the truths He revealed through the studying of His Word. Encourage your group toward the importance of the application journey and how transformation comes when we not only study the Word of God but act upon what He teaches us.

>**Day 2.** Luke 17:5-10

Leader Notes

Focal Points: (a.) Faith as a mustard seed. (b.) Jesus' expectation for disciples.

Revelation: Within the passages studied, ask the ladies to discuss the following: (a.) truths revealed about God's character, (b.) truths revealed that both ministered and encouraged their hearts, (c.) truths that brought conviction of sin and or need of change, (d.) truths revealing God's promises, (e.) truths revealed that restored hope.

Application: Foster to the ladies the importance of applying what they learned of the character of God and of the truths He revealed through the studying of His Word. Encourage your group toward the importance of the application journey and how transformation comes when we not only study the Word of God but act upon what He teaches us.

>Day 3. Luke 17:11-19

Leader Notes

Focal Points: (a.) The request from the ten lepers. (b.) The answer from Jesus to the lepers. (c.) Obedience and the miracle. (d.) The response from the nine and then from the one. (e.) The response of Jesus to the one: His question posed and the message given.

Revelation: Within the passages studied, ask the ladies to discuss the following: (a.) truths revealed about God's character, (b.) truths revealed that both ministered and encouraged their hearts, (c.) truths that brought conviction of sin and or need of change, (d.) truths revealing God's promises, (e.) truths revealed that restored hope.

Application: Foster to the ladies the importance of applying what they learned of the character of God and of the truths He revealed through the studying of His Word. Encourage your group toward the importance of the application journey and how transformation comes when we not only study the Word of God but act upon what He teaches us.

>Day 4. Luke 17:20-37

Leader Notes

Focal Points: (a.) The Pharisees question Jesus regarding the kingdom of God. (b.) The response of Jesus to the Pharisees. (c.) Jesus speaks of the second coming and to be prepared.

Revelation: Within the passages studied, ask the ladies to discuss the following: (a.) truths revealed about God's character, (b.) truths revealed that both ministered and encouraged their hearts, (c.) truths that brought conviction of sin and or need of change, (d.) truths revealing God's promises, (e.) truths revealed that restored hope.

Application: Foster to the ladies the importance of applying what they learned of the character of God and of the truths He revealed through the studying of His Word. Encourage your group toward the importance of the application journey and how transformation comes when we not only study the Word of God but act upon what He teaches us.

>Day 5. Feast on God's Truth:

a. Write out this week's scripture verse.
b. In what ways does this passage encourage your heart? How can you apply it to your life?

Looking Back at Truths Revealed: Spend time looking back over truths revealed for days 1–4. List below the truth that has resonated the most in your heart this week. (You can list more if you desire.)

Pass It On: Share the lessons you learned this week with your kids, your family, your friends, and those to whom God places in your path. Entrust to others what has been entrusted to you.

Notes

Week 18

Scripture Memory
"I tell you, this man went to his house justified rather than the other; for everyone who exalts himself will be humbled, but he who humbles himself will be exalted." (Luke 18:14)

Prayer
Lord Jesus, I come before you during this time of study, asking You to open my heart to hear Your Word and obey Your truth. In Jesus' name I pray, amen.

Scripture Reading By Day
*Truth Revealed: What truths did God reveal to you through today's scripture reading? What did God say to you—to your heart—as you read today's scripture?

*Truth Applied: How will you use what God revealed to you today in your daily life?

>**Day 1.** Luke 18:1-8

Leader Notes

Focal Points: (a.) Pray at all times and don't lose heart. (b.) The story of the judge and widow—persistence in prayer.

Revelation: Within the passages studied, ask the ladies to discuss the following: (a.) truths revealed about God's character, (b.) truths revealed that both ministered and encouraged their hearts, (c.) truths that brought conviction of sin and or need of change, (d.) truths revealing God's promises, (e.) truths revealed that restored hope.

Application: Foster to the ladies the importance of applying what they learned of the character of God and of the truths He revealed through the studying of His Word. Encourage your group toward the importance of the application journey and how transformation comes when we not only study the Word of God but act upon what He teaches us.

>**Day 2.** Luke 18:9-17

Leader Notes

Focal Points: (a.) The Pharisee's merit-based prayer and the tax collector's mercy-based prayer. (b.) Verse 14: what happens when one exalts himself and when one humbles himself? (c.) The kingdom of God and faith like a child.

Revelation: Within the passages studied, ask the ladies to discuss the following: (a.) truths revealed about God's character, (b.) truths revealed that both ministered and encouraged their hearts, (c.) truths that brought conviction of sin and or need of change, (d.) truths revealing God's promises, (e.) truths revealed that restored hope.

Application: Foster to the ladies the importance of applying what they learned of the character of God and of the truths He revealed through the studying of His Word. Encourage your group toward the importance of the application journey and how transformation comes when we not only study the Word of God but act upon what He teaches us.

>**Day 3.** Luke 18:18-34

Leader Notes

Focal Points: (a.) The dialogue between the rich young ruler and Jesus: the sin of the rich young ruler and the need for repentance. (b.) When one gives his or her life for the sake of the kingdom of God, they will be blessed. (c.) Jesus takes the twelve aside and gives them a message.

Revelation: Within the passages studied, ask the ladies to discuss the following: (a.) truths revealed about God's character, (b.) truths revealed that both ministered and encouraged their hearts, (c.) truths that brought conviction of sin and or need of change, (d.) truths revealing God's promises, (e.) truths revealed that restored hope.

Application: Foster to the ladies the importance of applying what they learned of the character of God and of the truths He revealed through the studying of His Word. Encourage your group toward the importance of the application journey and how transformation comes when we not only study the Word of God but act upon what He teaches us.

>**Day 4.** Luke 18:35-43

Leader Notes

Focal Points: (a.) The blind man calls out to Jesus for help. (b.) Individuals scold him, telling him to be quiet. (c.) The blind man continues to cry out to Jesus. (d.) The question Jesus posed to the man. (e.) The answer the blind man gave Jesus. (f.) The intervention of Jesus. (g.) The man's response to his healing and how others were impacted.

Revelation: Within the passages studied, ask the ladies to discuss the following: (a.) truths revealed about God's character, (b.) truths revealed that both ministered and encouraged their hearts, (c.) truths that brought conviction of sin and or need of change, (d.) truths revealing God's promises, (e.) truths revealed that restored hope.

Application: Foster to the ladies the importance of applying what they learned of the character of God and of the truths He revealed through the studying of His Word. Encourage your group toward the importance of the application journey and how transformation comes when we not only study the Word of God but act upon what He teaches us.

>**Day 5.** Feast on God's Truth:
   a.   Write out this week's scripture verse.
   b.   In what ways does this passage encourage your heart? How can you apply it to your life?

Looking Back at Truths Revealed: Spend time looking back over truths revealed for days 1–4. List below the truth that has resonated the most in your heart this week. (You can list more if you desire.)

Pass It On: Share the lessons you learned this week with your kids, your family, your friends, and those to whom God places in your path. Entrust to others what has been entrusted to you.

Notes

Week 19

Scripture Memory
"For the Son of Man has come to seek and to save that which was lost." (Luke 19:10)

Prayer
Lord Jesus, I come before you during this time of study, asking You to open my heart to hear Your Word and obey Your truth. In Jesus' name I pray, amen.

Scripture Reading By Day
*Truth Revealed: What truths did God reveal to you through today's scripture reading? What did God say to you—to your heart—as you read today's scripture?

*Truth Applied: How will you use what God revealed to you today in your daily life?

>**Day 1.** Luke 19:1-10

Leader Notes

Focal Points: (a.) The profession held by Zaccheus. (b.) The action taken by Zaccheus to see Jesus. (c.) The message given to Zaccheus by Jesus. (d.) The reaction from individuals over the action of Jesus. (e.) The message Zaccheus gives to the Lord of deeds he will carry out. (f.) The response of Jesus. (g.) For the Son of man has come to . . . ? (h.) Compare the circumstances and response of Zaccheus vs. the rich young ruler.

Revelation: Within the passages studied, ask the ladies to discuss the following: (a.) truths revealed about God's character, (b.) truths revealed that both ministered and encouraged their hearts, (c.) truths that brought conviction of sin and or need of change, (d.) truths revealing God's promises, (e.) truths revealed that restored hope.

Application: Foster to the ladies the importance of applying what they learned of the character of God and of the truths He revealed through the studying of His Word. Encourage your group toward the importance of the application journey and how transformation comes when we not only study the Word of God but act upon what He teaches us.

>**Day 2.** Luke 19:11-27

Leader Notes

Focal Points: (a.) The teaching of Jesus regarding the coming kingdom of God. (b.) Who the nobleman represented and who the citizens are. (c.) Faithful servants vs. unfaithful servants.

Revelation: Within the passages studied, ask the ladies to discuss the following: (a.) truths revealed about God's character, (b.) truths revealed that both ministered and encouraged their hearts, (c.) truths that brought conviction of sin and or need of change, (d.) truths revealing God's promises, (e.) truths revealed that restored hope.

Application: Foster to the ladies the importance of applying what they learned of the character of God and of the truths He revealed through the studying of His Word. Encourage your group toward the importance of the application journey and how transformation comes when we not only study the Word of God but act upon what He teaches us.

>**Day 3.** Luke 19:28-44

Leader Notes

Focal Points: (a.) The instructions given by Jesus to His disciples. (b.) The triumphal entry, shouts from the crowd of the disciples, and the fulfillment of prophecy. (c.) Message from the Pharisees and the response from Jesus. (d.) When Jesus approached Jerusalem, He saw the city, and He wept. (e.) His message.

Revelation: Within the passages studied, ask the ladies to discuss the following: (a.) truths revealed about God's character, (b.) truths revealed that both ministered and encouraged their hearts, (c.) truths that brought conviction of sin and or need of change, (d.) truths revealing God's promises, (e.) truths revealed that restored hope.

Application: Foster to the ladies the importance of applying what they learned of the character of God and of the truths He revealed through the studying of His Word. Encourage your group toward the importance of the application journey and how transformation comes when we not only study the Word of God but act upon what He teaches us.

>**Day 4.** Luke 19:45-48

Leader Notes

Focal Points: (a.) Jesus enters the temple. (b.) The reaction of Jesus toward those selling in the temple; his message. (c.) Jesus continued to teach daily in the temple. (d.) The thoughts/plans of the chief priests, scribes, and leading men. (e.) The people's response to the teaching of Jesus.

Revelation: Within the passages studied, ask the ladies to discuss the following: (a.) truths revealed about God's character, (b.) truths revealed that both ministered and encouraged their hearts, (c.) truths that brought conviction of sin and or need of change, (d.) truths revealing God's promises, (e.) truths revealed that restored hope.

Application: Foster to the ladies the importance of applying what they learned of the character of God and of the truths He revealed through the studying of His Word. Encourage your group toward the importance of the application journey and how transformation comes when we not only study the Word of God but act upon what He teaches us.

>**Day 5.** Feast on God's Truth:
   a. Write out this week's scripture verse.
   b. In what ways does this passage encourage your heart? How can you apply it to your life?

Looking Back at Truths Revealed: Spend time looking back over truths revealed for days 1–4. List below the truth that has resonated the most in your heart this week. (You can list more if you desire.)

Pass It On: Share the lessons you learned this week with your kids, your family, your friends, and those to whom God places in your path. Entrust to others what has been entrusted to you.

Notes

Week 20

Scripture Memory
And He said to them, "Then render to Caesar the things that are Caesar's, and to God the things that are God's." (Luke 20:25)

Prayer
Lord Jesus, I come before you during this time of study, asking You to open my heart to hear Your Word and obey Your truth. In Jesus' name I pray, amen.

Scripture Reading By Day
*Truth Revealed: What truths did God reveal to you through today's scripture reading? What did God say to you—to your heart—as you read today's scripture?

*Truth Applied: How will you use what God revealed to you today in your daily life?

>**Day 1.** Luke 20:1-8

Leader Notes

Focal Points: (a.) The dialogue between Jesus and those questioning His authority as the Son of God.

Revelation: Within the passages studied, ask the ladies to discuss the following: (a.) truths revealed about God's character, (b.) truths revealed that both ministered and encouraged their hearts, (c.) truths that brought conviction of sin and or need of change, (d.) truths revealing God's promises, (e.) truths revealed that restored hope.

Application: Foster to the ladies the importance of applying what they learned of the character of God and of the truths He revealed through the studying of His Word. Encourage your group toward the importance of the application journey and how transformation comes when we not only study the Word of God but act upon what He teaches us.

>**Day 2.** Luke 20:9-18

Leader Notes

Focal Points: (a.) Jesus' parable of the vine growers—who the vineyard owner is and who the vine growers were. (b.) The action of the vine growers toward the vineyard owner's slaves and son. (c.) The significance of vss. 17-18 in regard to this parable.

Revelation: Within the passages studied, ask the ladies to discuss the following: (a.) truths revealed about God's character, (b.) truths revealed that both ministered and encouraged their hearts, (c.) truths that brought conviction of sin and or need of change, (d.) truths revealing God's promises, (e.) truths revealed that restored hope.

Application: Foster to the ladies the importance of applying what they learned of the character of God and of the truths He revealed through the studying of His Word. Encourage your group toward the importance of the application journey and how transformation comes when we not only study the Word of God but act upon what He teaches us.

>**Day 3.** Luke 20:19-26

Leader Notes

Focal Points: (a.) Spies sent, pretending to be righteous for evil intent toward Jesus. (b.) The question posed to Jesus about paying taxes to Caesar. (c.) Jesus detects their trickery. (d.) The response of Jesus. (e.) Individuals amazed at the answer given by Jesus.

Revelation: Within the passages studied, ask the ladies to discuss the following: (a.) truths revealed about God's character, (b.) truths revealed that both ministered and encouraged their hearts, (c.) truths that brought conviction of sin and or need of change, (d.) truths revealing God's promises, (e.) truths revealed that restored hope.

Application: Foster to the ladies the importance of applying what they learned of the character of God and of the truths He revealed through the studying of His Word. Encourage your group toward the importance of the application journey and how transformation comes when we not only study the Word of God but act upon what He teaches us.

>**Day 4.** Luke 20:27-47

Leader Notes

Focal Points: (a.) The Sadducees who didn't believe in the resurrection test Jesus with questions. (b.) Jesus corrects the Sadducees. (c.) Christ challenged and reprimanded the scribes for their unbelief and pride.

Revelation: Within the passages studied, ask the ladies to discuss the following: (a.) truths revealed about God's character, (b.) truths revealed that both ministered and encouraged their hearts, (c.) truths that brought conviction of sin and or need of change, (d.) truths revealing God's promises, (e.) truths revealed that restored hope.

Application: Foster to the ladies the importance of applying what they learned of the character of God and of the truths He revealed through the studying of His Word. Encourage your group toward the importance of the application journey and how transformation comes when we not only study the Word of God but act upon what He teaches us.

>**Day 5.** Feast on God's Truth:

   a.   Write out this week's scripture verse.
   b.   In what ways does this passage encourage your heart? How can you apply it to your life?

Looking Back at Truths Revealed: Spend time looking back over truths revealed for days 1–4. List below the truth that has resonated the most in your heart this week. (You can list more if you desire.)

Pass It On: Share the lessons you learned this week with your kids, your family, your friends, and those to whom God places in your path. Entrust to others what has been entrusted to you.

Notes

Week 21

Scripture Memory
"Then they will see the Son of Man coming in a cloud with power and great glory." (Luke 21:27)

Prayer
Lord Jesus, I come before you during this time of study, asking You to open my heart to hear Your Word and obey Your truth. In Jesus' name I pray, amen.

Scripture Reading By Day
*Truth Revealed: What truths did God reveal to you through today's scripture reading? What did God say to you—to your heart—as you read today's scripture?

*Truth Applied: How will you use what God revealed to you today in your daily life?

>**Day 1.** Luke 21:1-4

Leader Notes

Focal Points: (a.) The rich gifts vs. the widow's gift placed into the treasury. (b.) Sacrificial giving and the true heart condition.

Revelation: Within the passages studied, ask the ladies to discuss the following: (a.) truths revealed about God's character, (b.) truths revealed that both ministered and encouraged their hearts, (c.) truths that brought conviction of sin and or need of change, (d.) truths revealing God's promises, (e.) truths revealed that restored hope.

Application: Foster to the ladies the importance of applying what they learned of the character of God and of the truths He revealed through the studying of His Word. Encourage your group toward the importance of the application journey and how transformation comes when we not only study the Word of God but act upon what He teaches us.

>**Day 2.** Luke 21:5-19

Leader Notes

Focal Points: (a.) Jesus shares about the signs of things to come. (b.) "It will lead to an opportunity for your testimony." (c.) The promise of wisdom and utterance. (d.) Following Jesus, betrayals, hatred, and protection.

Revelation: Within the passages studied, ask the ladies to discuss the following: (a.) truths revealed about God's character, (b.) truths revealed that both ministered and encouraged their hearts, (c.) truths that brought conviction of sin and or need of change, (d.) truths revealing God's promises, (e.) truths revealed that restored hope.

Application: Foster to the ladies the importance of applying what they learned of the character of God and of the truths He revealed through the studying of His Word. Encourage your group toward the importance of the application journey and how transformation comes when we not only study the Word of God but act upon what He teaches us.

>**Day 3.** Luke 21:20-24

Leader Notes

Focal Points: (a.) Continuation of things to come, spoken by Jesus. (b.) The times of the Gentiles to be fulfilled.

Revelation: Within the passages studied, ask the ladies to discuss the following: (a.) truths revealed about God's character, (b.) truths revealed that both ministered and encouraged their hearts, (c.) truths that brought conviction of sin and or need of change, (d.) truths revealing God's promises, (e.) truths revealed that restored hope.

Application: Foster to the ladies the importance of applying what they learned of the character of God and of the truths He revealed through the studying of His Word. Encourage your group toward the importance of the application journey and how transformation comes when we not only study the Word of God but act upon what He teaches us.

>**Day 4.** Luke 21:25-38

Leader Notes

Focal Points: (a.) The Son of Man coming and redemption is drawing near. (b.) Jesus gives the parable explaining the nearness of the kingdom of God. (c.) Keep alert at all times.

Revelation: Within the passages studied, ask the ladies to discuss the following: (a.) truths revealed about God's character, (b.) truths revealed that both ministered and encouraged their hearts, (c.) truths that brought conviction of sin and or need of change, (d.) truths revealing God's promises, (e.) truths revealed that restored hope.

Application: Foster to the ladies the importance of applying what they learned of the character of God and of the truths He revealed through the studying of His Word. Encourage your group toward the importance of the application journey and how transformation comes when we not only study the Word of God but act upon what He teaches us.

>**Day 5.** Feast on God's Truth:
   a.   Write out this week's scripture verse.
   b.   In what ways does this passage encourage your heart? How can you apply it to your life?

Looking Back at Truths Revealed: Spend time looking back over truths revealed for days 1–4. List below the truth that has resonated the most in your heart this week. (You can list more if you desire.)

Pass It On: Share the lessons you learned this week with your kids, your family, your friends, and those to whom God places in your path. Entrust to others what has been entrusted to you.

Notes

Week 22

Scripture Memory
And He withdrew from them about a stone's throw, and He knelt down and began to pray, saying, "Father, if You are willing, remove this cup from Me; yet not My will, but Yours be done."
(Luke 22:41-42)

Prayer
Lord Jesus, I come before you during this time of study, asking You to open my heart to hear Your Word and obey Your truth. In Jesus' name I pray, amen.

Scripture Reading By Day
__Truth Revealed:__ What truths did God reveal to you through today's scripture reading? What did God say to you—to your heart—as you read today's scripture?

__Truth Applied:__ How will you use what God revealed to you today in your daily life?

>**Day 1.** Luke 22:1-23

Leader Notes

Focal Points: (a.) The betrayal of Jesus planned. (b.) Judas discusses his betrayal of Jesus and looks for opportunity to carry it out. (c.) Preparation of the Passover and the Passover observed; the significance of the Passover observed with Jesus (old covenant/new covenant).

Revelation: Within the passages studied, ask the ladies to discuss the following: (a.) truths revealed about God's character, (b.) truths revealed that both ministered and encouraged their hearts, (c.) truths that brought conviction of sin and or need of change, (d.) truths revealing God's promises, (e.) truths revealed that restored hope.

Application: Foster to the ladies the importance of applying what they learned of the character of God and of the truths He revealed through the studying of His Word. Encourage your group toward the importance of the application journey and how transformation comes when we not only study the Word of God but act upon what He teaches us.

>**Day 2.** Luke 22:24-38

Leader Notes

Focal Points: (a.) The dispute: who is the greatest? The answer from Jesus. (b.) Jesus addresses those who stood by Him—blessings promised. (c.) The permission given to Satan to sift Peter like wheat and the prayer of Jesus for Peter. (d.) Peter's response. (e.) Peter's denial announced. (f.) Jesus prepares His disciples for what is ahead.

Revelation: Within the passages studied, ask the ladies to discuss the following: (a.) truths revealed about God's character, (b.) truths revealed that both ministered and encouraged their hearts, (c.) truths that brought conviction of sin and or need of change, (d.) truths revealing God's promises, (e.) truths revealed that restored hope.

Application: Foster to the ladies the importance of applying what they learned of the character of God and of the truths He revealed through the studying of His Word. Encourage your group toward the importance of the application journey and how transformation comes when we not only study the Word of God but act upon what He teaches us.

Notes

>**Day 3.** Luke 22:39-53

Leader Notes

Focal Points: (a.) The Garden of Gethsemane. (b.) The prayer of Jesus. (c.) Jesus is strengthened. (d.) His sweat becomes like drops of blood. (e.) Disciples had fallen asleep from sorrow. (f.) The betrayal of Jesus.

Revelation: Within the passages studied, ask the ladies to discuss the following: (a.) truths revealed about God's character, (b.) truths revealed that both ministered and encouraged their hearts, (c.) truths that brought conviction of sin and or need of change, (d.) truths revealing God's promises, (e.) truths revealed that restored hope.

Application: Foster to the ladies the importance of applying what they learned of the character of God and of the truths He revealed through the studying of His Word. Encourage your group toward the importance of the application journey and how transformation comes when we not only study the Word of God but act upon what He teaches us.

>**Day 4.** Luke 22:54-71

Leader Notes

Focal Points: (a.) Peter's denial. (b.) The rooster crows, and Jesus turns and looks at Peter. (c.) Peter remembers, and Peter wept. (d.) Jesus mocked and beaten. (e.) Jesus questioned, and Jesus responds.

Revelation: Within the passages studied, ask the ladies to discuss the following: (a.) truths revealed about God's character, (b.) truths revealed that both ministered and encouraged their hearts, (c.) truths that brought conviction of sin and or need of change, (d.) truths revealing God's promises, (e.) truths revealed that restored hope.

Application: Foster to the ladies the importance of applying what they learned of the character of God and of the truths He revealed through the studying of His Word. Encourage your group toward the importance of the application journey and how transformation comes when we not only study the Word of God but act upon what He teaches us.

>**Day 5.** Feast on God's Truth:
   a. Write out this week's scripture verse.
   b. In what ways does this passage encourage your heart? How can you apply it to your life?

Looking Back at Truths Revealed: Spend time looking back over truths revealed for days 1–4. List below the truth that has resonated the most in your heart this week. (You can list more if you desire.)

Pass It On: Share the lessons you learned this week with your kids, your family, your friends, and those to whom God places in your path. Entrust to others what has been entrusted to you.

Notes

Week 23

Scripture Memory

But Jesus was saying, "Father, forgive them; for they do not know what they are doing." And they cast lots, dividing up His garments among themselves. (Luke 23:34)

Prayer

Lord Jesus, I come before you during this time of study, asking You to open my heart to hear Your Word and obey Your truth. In Jesus' name I pray, amen.

Scripture Reading By Day

Truth Revealed: What truths did God reveal to you through today's scripture reading? What did God say to you—to your heart—as you read today's scripture?

Truth Applied: How will you use what God revealed to you today in your daily life?

>**Day 1.** Luke 23:1-25

Leader Notes

Focal Points: (a.) Pilate and Jesus. (b.) Herod and Jesus. (c.) Pilate and Jesus—the shouts, "Crucify Him." (d.) Pilate delivers Jesus over to be crucified.

Revelation: Within the passages studied, ask the ladies to discuss the following: (a.) truths revealed about God's character, (b.) truths revealed that both ministered and encouraged their hearts, (c.) truths that brought conviction of sin and or need of change, (d.) truths revealing God's promises, (e.) truths revealed that restored hope.

Application: Foster to the ladies the importance of applying what they learned of the character of God and of the truths He revealed through the studying of His Word. Encourage your group toward the importance of the application journey and how transformation comes when we not only study the Word of God but act upon what He teaches us.

>**Day 2.** Luke 23:26-31

Leader Notes

Focal Points: (a.) Simon carries the cross. (b.) People mourn and lament Jesus. (c.) The message spoken by Jesus to those mourning.

Revelation: Within the passages studied, ask the ladies to discuss the following: (a.) truths revealed about God's character, (b.) truths revealed that both ministered and encouraged their hearts, (c.) truths that brought conviction of sin and or need of change, (d.) truths revealing God's promises, (e.) truths revealed that restored hope.

Application: Foster to the ladies the importance of applying what they learned of the character of God and of the truths He revealed through the studying of His Word. Encourage your group toward the importance of the application journey and how transformation comes when we not only study the Word of God but act upon what He teaches us.

>Day 3. Luke 23:32-49

Leader Notes

Focal Points: (a.) Jesus is crucified, and His response thereof. (b.) Jesus is mocked. (c.) The criminal's request: "Jesus, remember me." (d.) The response of Jesus to the criminal's petition. (e.) Jesus breathes His last. (f.) The response of the Centurion.

Revelation: Within the passages studied, ask the ladies to discuss the following: (a.) truths revealed about God's character, (b.) truths revealed that both ministered and encouraged their hearts, (c.) truths that brought conviction of sin and or need of change, (d.) truths revealing God's promises, (e.) truths revealed that restored hope.

Application: Foster to the ladies the importance of applying what they learned of the character of God and of the truths He revealed through the studying of His Word. Encourage your group toward the importance of the application journey and how transformation comes when we not only study the Word of God but act upon what He teaches us.

>Day 4. Luke 23:50-56

Leader Notes

Focal Points: (a.) The request made by Joseph to Pilate. (b.) The fulfillment of prophecy and Joseph lays Jesus in the tomb. (c.) The women prepare spices and perfume.

Revelation: Within the passages studied, ask the ladies to discuss the following: (a.) truths revealed about God's character, (b.) truths revealed that both ministered and encouraged their hearts, (c.) truths that brought conviction of sin and or need of change, (d.) truths revealing God's promises, (e.) truths revealed that restored hope.

Application: Foster to the ladies the importance of applying what they learned of the character of God and of the truths He revealed through the studying of His Word. Encourage your group toward the importance of the application journey and how transformation comes when we not only study the Word of God but act upon what He teaches us.

>Day 5. Feast on God's Truth:
a.   Write out this week's scripture verse.
b.   In what ways does this passage encourage your heart? How can you apply it to your life?

Looking Back at Truths Revealed: Spend time looking back over truths revealed for days 1–4. List below the truth that has resonated the most in your heart this week. (You can list more if you desire.)

Pass It On: Share the lessons you learned this week with your kids, your family, your friends, and those to whom God places in your path. Entrust to others what has been entrusted to you.

Notes

Week 24

Scripture Memory
Then He opened their minds to understand the Scriptures. (Luke 24:45)

Prayer
Lord Jesus, I come before you during this time of study, asking You to open my heart to hear Your Word and obey Your truth. In Jesus' name I pray, amen.

Scripture Reading By Day
Truth Revealed: What truths did God reveal to you through today's scripture reading? What did God say to you—to your heart—as you read today's scripture?

Truth Applied: How will you use what God revealed to you today in your daily life?

>**Day 1.** Luke 24:1-12

Leader Notes

Focal Points: (a.) The stone rolled away. (b.) Women arrive first; the scene inside the tomb. (c.) The message given by the two men. (d.) News reported to others about what had taken place; the response. (e.) Peter runs to the tomb.

Revelation: Within the passages studied, ask the ladies to discuss the following: (a.) truths revealed about God's character, (b.) truths revealed that both ministered and encouraged their hearts, (c.) truths that brought conviction of sin and or need of change, (d.) truths revealing God's promises, (e.) truths revealed that restored hope.

Application: Foster to the ladies the importance of applying what they learned of the character of God and of the truths He revealed through the studying of His Word. Encourage your group toward the importance of the application journey and how transformation comes when we not only study the Word of God but act upon what He teaches us.

>**Day 2.** Luke 24:13-35

Leader Notes

Focal Points: (a.) The conversation between the risen Christ and those traveling to Emmaus. (b.) Dashed hopes. (c.) The teaching of Jesus regarding Himself in the scriptures. (d.) The breaking of bread and the recognition of Christ. (e.) Jesus vanishes and the response of others. (f.) The news spreads.

Revelation: Within the passages studied, ask the ladies to discuss the following: (a.) truths revealed about God's character, (b.) truths revealed that both ministered and encouraged their hearts, (c.) truths that brought conviction of sin and or need of change, (d.) truths revealing God's promises, (e.) truths revealed that restored hope.

Application: Foster to the ladies the importance of applying what they learned of the character of God and of the truths He revealed through the studying of His Word. Encourage your group toward the importance of the application journey and how transformation comes when we not only study the Word of God but act upon what He teaches us.

Notes

>**Day 3.** Luke 24:36-49

Leader Notes

Focal Points: (a.) The appearance of Jesus who speaks peace. (b.) The response from others to His appearance. (c.) Jesus responds to their fear. (d.) Jesus affirms the Word and opens the minds of the disciples to the scriptures; the Great Commission; the promise of the Spirit.

Revelation: Within the passages studied, ask the ladies to discuss the following: (a.) truths revealed about God's character, (b.) truths revealed that both ministered and encouraged their hearts, (c.) truths that brought conviction of sin and or need of change, (d.) truths revealing God's promises, (e.) truths revealed that restored hope.

Application: Foster to the ladies the importance of applying what they learned of the character of God and of the truths He revealed through the studying of His Word. Encourage your group toward the importance of the application journey and how transformation comes when we not only study the Word of God but act upon what He teaches us.

>**Day 4.** Luke 24:50-53

Leader Notes

Focal Points: (a.) Jesus ascended and the disciples worshipped.

Revelation: Within the passages studied, ask the ladies to discuss the following: (a.) truths revealed about God's character, (b.) truths revealed that both ministered and encouraged their hearts, (c.) truths that brought conviction of sin and or need of change, (d.) truths revealing God's promises, (e.) truths revealed that restored hope.

Application: Foster to the ladies the importance of applying what they learned of the character of God and of the truths He revealed through the studying of His Word. Encourage your group toward the importance of the application journey and how transformation comes when we not only study the Word of God but act upon what He teaches us.

>**Day 5.** Feast on God's Truth:
  a. Write out this week's scripture verse.
  b. In what ways does this passage encourage your heart? How can you apply it to your life?

Looking Back at Truths Revealed: Spend time looking back over truths revealed for days 1–4. List below the truth that has resonated the most in your heart this week. (You can list more if you desire.)

Pass It On: Share the lessons you learned this week with your kids, your family, your friends, and those to whom God places in your path. Entrust to others what has been entrusted to you.

More from Dr. O'Shea Lowery

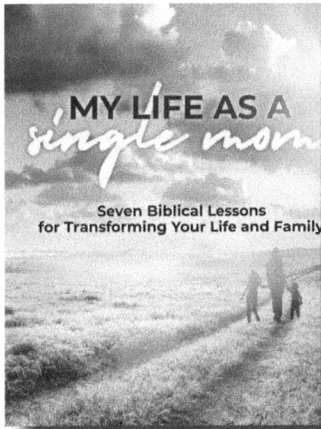

My Life as a Single Mom
Seven Biblical Lessons for Transforming Your Life and Family

God created you with a unique purpose and plan.

Our journeys take us through crossroads where decisions must be made, to mountaintops where victories are celebrated, and to detours where a once stable voyage suddenly takes a new turn. Much of the time, the most difficult part is living through all the unknowns as we try to discover what God's plan is.

My Life as a Single Mom: Seven Biblical Lessons for Transforming Your Life and Family is a seven-week individual study composed of collective works from God's Word and from others who lived centuries before. This study is geared toward single mothers but is an essential resource for all women, addressing fundamental truths every woman needs to walk in her faith. Through His Word, God gives principles to instruct her, wisdom to guide her, and truths to help her as she moves forward on the journey that has been entrusted to her.

Explore More from Innovo Publishing

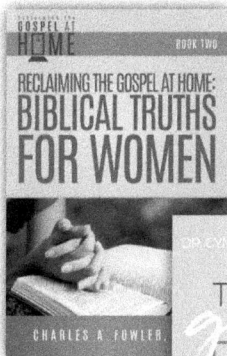

Biblical Truths for Women
by Charles A. Fowler

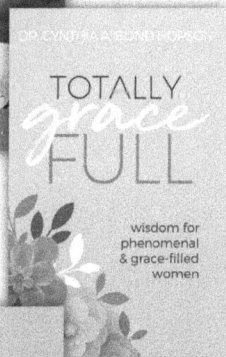

Totally GraceFULL
by Cynthia Hopson

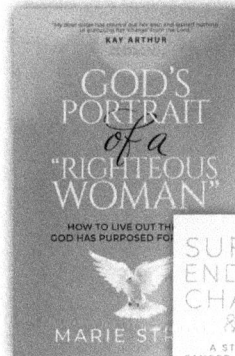

New Every Morning
by Adrian Rogers

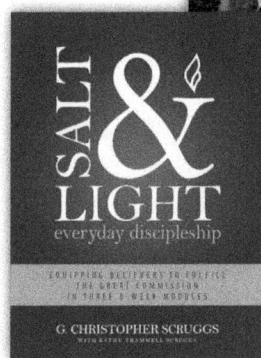

God's Portrait of a "Righteous Woman"
by Marie Strain

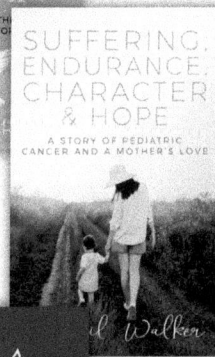

Suffering, Endurance, Character & Hope
by Abigail Walker

Salt & Light: Everyday Discipleship
by Christopher Scruggs